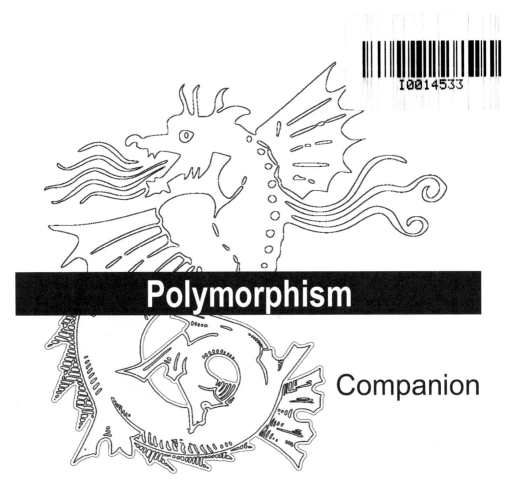

Polymorphism

Companion

Joseph Bergin, Ph.D.

Polymorphism

Companion

Joseph Bergin, Ph. D.

Published by Slant Flying Press, 2015

ISBN 978-1-940113-06-7

Cover: Great Peng Mounts the Sky. Great Peng is a mythical Chinese monster that is both fish and bird. The cover image represents Peng in its bird aspect. It is *Wing of the Peng*, from the Kyōka Hyaku Monogatari manuscript of 1852.

Printed: September 27, 2015

Introduction

There are some things I didn't include in *Polymorphism: As It Is Played* to keep the book short and simple. It provides only the main line path through the material. Here I will provide additional information, hints, exercises, ideas, tricks, and rants. I also admit that I conceived and built the calculator project myself. I can't blame my students for any flaws. I'll reveal a few flaws here, in fact. This is not a correction to the first book, as the flaws are instructive to the reader, and aid learning when discovered and followed up. There are also some important ideas implicit in the code and the process explained in *Polymorphism* that some might miss. They can be vital lessons for the budding programmer. The project described there was used several times over the years. The resulting code was a bit different each time.

I often told my students that it wasn't my job to teach them what I *knew*, since much of that was already obsolete, even garbage. Instead it was to show them how I *thought*. How I thought about problems, solutions, coding, being a success, etc. I don't claim my thought process is perfect, but it is *experienced*, at least. I even know details of the hidden bit. We needed that in the long-ago past.

It is also my job to *set the conditions* for learning, and this usually means giving students interesting and difficult problems to solve. Here we will try to provide some entertaining exercises, though a few are just hidden in questions, as was done in *Polymorphism*.

Here you will find additional thoughts about polymorphism as well as several case-study projects that might be explored. There are more stories for the calculator. There are other calculators. There are other projects presented as stories for your enjoyment. There is code that might serve as a basis for transformation to a more polymorphic form, or just be studied, as it is interesting in itself.

However, this is a personal view. I'll write about my personal coding style and why I like it. I'll talk about why I sometimes deviate from the standard forms. I'll admit to inconsistency. Ah well. Not perfect. Good, but not perfect.

Acknowledgements

OpenClipArt.org for the images used here, other than the cover

    Gubrww2

    Liftarn: www.interface1.net.webloc

Michael Goldweber gave important feedback on the first book that has influenced what I've done here.

Rinaldo DiGeorgio reminded me that my views on pair programming aren't universally held.

Richard Pattis read an earlier version and made valuable comments that I've tried to incorporate. He provides a sanity check that I often need.

This book is dedicated to my family, especially my wife. Thanks for your patience.

Additional Information about this Companion can be found at:
    http://csis.pace.edu/~bergin/polymorphismCompanionBook.

Many references will be made to the earlier book: *Polymorphism: As It Is Played.*

> The hoped-for audience is primarily novices and instructors of novices. Novice instructors are especially welcome here.

Contents

programming …

bringing a new world

into life

Sorry, not haiku
maybe close but not so near
fun to play with though

Joseph Bergin

1 + 1 < 2

Two people working together are more powerful than those same two people working separately! Is that true? Often enough it is. If nothing else, the task can be more pleasant. I've had an image in my mind for a while of a vast office full of cubicles, one person each, all working on different parts of the same project, and everyone simultaneously stuck. However, everyone's missing bit of knowledge is held by someone else in another cubicle. Or even everyone else.

Managers who have never been developers worry that they are spending twice as much as required when programmers work in pairs, but it turns out not to be the case. Quality of code goes up with pair programming and quantity of code written doesn't go down, or not by enough to matter, anyway [Williams and Kessler].

I've seen pairing work in the industrial domain and I find it equally important in teaching and learning. I've given up the idea that everything the student learns should come out of my mouth. Students can, and do, help each other learn. I've also given up thinking that each student should learn exactly the same thing in the same way. Yes, they *will* learn differently. They *will*, on occasion, slack and let others carry the weight. But each student can contribute to a pair or team. If you want students to *want* to learn then you need to find ways to motivate them to learn. If you don't, many won't. I assume that doesn't surprise you, and that if you teach then you think a lot about motivation, and not with the stick.

Students need to learn a lot of things beyond technical details. The most important, of course, is how to live their lives. Among the *professional* skills required is communication, both speaking and writing. Even the extremely introverted benefit from situations in which they need to interact outside their natural comfort zone. But people who simply refuse to work with others or who refuse to gain the skill to do so are much less valuable to an employer. Occasionally a true *prima donna* comes along to test that idea. But they are very rare.

1

Students who are pair programming can test one another's understanding of a Story or, more generally, of a topic. They can come to a consensus about the meaning of a concept, or decide that neither has a good grasp, and that it is time to visit the professor. They can challenge each other, in a good way, to excel. Or, they can grate on each other, of course. In the professional world, pairing is often used to bring new hires up to speed quickly. They *navigate* for a while until they start to get the feel of the project. Then they *drive* for relatively simple features. This is much better than sitting them in a corner reading already-obsolete documentation.

One aspect of pairing, in practice, is the idea that the Driver naturally takes a tactical view of the code, needing to get the details right, while the Navigator takes the strategic, big picture, view. The navigator can remind the driver of decisions made earlier, for example, which keeps the coding consistent. A good navigator will be solving the problems along with the driver and when he or she notices a divergence of thought about the solution, will raise the issue. A short discussion can make the product better, and can also make the learning deeper.

Explaining something to another person that you barely understand yourself is often a good way to deepen your understanding. Pairing helps here, as well, especially if you have to try to explain ugly code. Explaining in general is a useful skill.

Asking questions is another important skill. Some people assume that they understand something when they don't. Some people are afraid to ask for help. Pairing helps here, as well. A rule that you might impose on student pairs is that when they disagree on something important, they should bring the instructor into the conversation. Small disagreements are usually resolved by letting the driver drive. Not every disagreement leads to disaster. Testing, when used, keeps you pretty close to the required path in any case. And even if they go wrong, refactoring is a valuable skill.

Students can benefit greatly from having an always-on public forum in which they can ask questions. A class-wide mailing list works well for this, as the students don't need to be connected continuously to be able to take part. Students should be encouraged to ask questions there and to bring their concerns, other than personal issues. But they should also be encouraged to answer questions posed by others. Some questions and answers will be a surprise to some students, especially if they missed something earlier. This can permit them to fill in the gaps. You need to monitor the conversations, of course, and correct any misinformation soon after it appears.

Often enough, a question raised in a forum will remind you that you need to discuss something in class. Perhaps you mis-spoke, or didn't cover a topic in sufficient detail. You can even post relatively long replies, mini-lectures, to the mailing list as needed.

Another useful item is a public FAQ (Frequently Asked Questions) page on a web site. Many questions that students have can be answered here. Many questions that students have recur each time you teach the course. So, over time, you provide an increasingly valuable resource to the students and also reduce the number of questions you get asked. If you frequently update the FAQ, all the better.

Another vital skill of any professional is the ability to write clearly. My colleague, Fred Grossman, and I have experimented in Pair Writing. Pairs are tasked with developing some topic. We made it fun by having them write Fairy Tales. We first had them spend a few minutes writing alone. Then they paired off and wrote a similar assignment. The pair versions were invariably more creative. More seriously, however, you could task pairs of students with writing on some topic raised by a question. The results might wind up in your FAQ. Documenting a project is another good pair task.

So is it true that pair programming is *always* the best way? A Google search for something like "Why not pair programming?" will be instructive. In fact, I do most of my programming alone, but that isn't from choice. I'm normally a team of one and don't have a colleague with which to share the work. Sometimes it leads me to write terrible code. I've also been in team situations in which pairing was not used and it let to serious trouble. Testing is all the more important in such cases.

But if you haven't tried pairing, don't think that you will necessarily hate it. That is too common an initial response.

Coding Ideas and Style

The experienced Java programmer, and many instructors, may have noticed that I use a somewhat non-standard coding style. It isn't accidental. I'd like to say a bit about why I think that style is useful, even important. Be warned that this is something of a rant.

First, I try to never abbreviate any word in a program. I'll spell out even long words completely. This is most important when the name has large scope. I've found, that in a lifetime of programming, abbreviating costs you time and effort. You will forget how you spell all but the most common and standard abbreviations. So, rather than having to look back to check on your spelling of a term, you just spell it correctly (or at least, consistently) each time. Modern IDEs like Eclipse will provide spelling completion in any case, so long words seldom need to be typed out. And it isn't typing that makes programming hard, or slow, as I mentioned in PAIIP. Oh, dear. I just abbreviated, didn't I. Oh well. I'll just refer to the earlier book as *Polymorphism* from now on.

Next, is that I always try to use an *intention revealing name*, even in the simplest of cases, such as a counting FOR loop (*What* are you counting, anyway?) or a parameter to be used only once. Thus, Julie and Zahid had a discussion about whether an argument should be simply *n*, or something more meaningful in the problem space: *keyValue*. I'm not fanatical about this, but I find it helpful overall. I usually relent for array subscripts determined by FOR loops. This reveals my FORTRAN background, of course.

Ward Cunningham, the inventor of the wiki and lots of other interesting things, once said that every programmer should keep a thesaurus next to the computer. I've found that to be very useful.

Related to the above, I generally try to find names from the problem space, not the solution space. For example a flag, if used shouldn't be named *flag*, nor a field, *field*, etc. Of course that sounds silly. The name of a flag should indicate the event that happened, perhaps *plusPressed*.

And, related to that, and more controversial, I try to use a single name for a concept however it appears in the program, even if I need to use the same name for a class, method, field, etc. For example, if I need a field named *size* for an object in class GumBall, I will likely write the constructor as

```
public GumBall(int size){
    this.size = size;
}
```

using *size* for both the field and the parameter of the constructor. If *size* needs an accessor, I'll write it as

```
public size(){
    return this.size;
{
```

One name for each concept. Then I don't need to make up unique names for the various aspects of the concept just because they represent different things in the code. I think of *this* as my friend.

And, you are unlikely to ever see anything like *getSize* and *setSize* in my code. I find that convention counterproductive, even abominable. One simple reason is aesthetic. "John, what is the getTime?" Stupid, stupid, stupid. <\rant>

But the real reason is much more important. If you write a lot of code using this convention, you are likely to read it thinking entirely in terms of the implementations of things, the fields, rather than the abstractions that you are trying to build. If you do this, you will start to think at too low a level. You would really like to think about your program in terms of the problem space and the natural concepts there, but this ugly convention forces you to think in terms of the implementation. So, use the names from the problem space, not from geek-space.

I once gave some students an exercise to build a project of their own design. As part of the initial startup for the project, I asked the students to estimate how many classes they thought they would need and how many methods. I didn't expect accuracy, but just wanted them to begin to think about estimating things. One student, however, for the number of methods, did an analysis of all the fields he would need in the project and then doubled that for the number of methods. A getter and a setter for each variable.

We had a discussion about that, but in the end, his project really developed no abstractions. He just programmed in Java with the variables as if it had been assembly language.

So, I try to write the code in terms of the abstractions, not the fields with which they are implemented. Partly for this reason, when lecturing I use the terms *accessor* and *mutator* rather than getter and setter. An accessor yields some information from an object, not necessarily a field. A mutator changes the state of the computation in some way, not necessarily by giving a field a new value.

And I try, most of the time, to avoid writing methods that change the state but also yield information: accesso-mutators. Sometimes it is helpful, though, as when inserting into a Map but getting back the old value associated with the key at the same time. But, I write such methods only rarely. Separation of concerns is normally a better choice.

It also aids conversation within a team when class names are nouns and noun phrases, since classes create *things*, and are descriptions of *things*: objects. Also, should you name your class GumBall or GumballMaker? What does the class *describe*? If gum balls, then call it GumBall. Likewise, mutators should have verb/verb phrase names describing the action performed. Accessors should have names that are nouns and noun phrases, describing the returned information. Then the name fit into ordinary sentences in a discussion without awkward phrasing. In *Polymorphism* we have an odd case. The display of the calculator was called *display*. That is both a verb and a noun. Does display() *do* something? Or does it *return* something? Julie and Zahid didn't comment on that, nor did Dr. J raise the issue at the time, but, if you don't remember that the method is an accessor, you will write incorrect code for a bit until you refresh your own memory. Thanks to Richard Pattis for pointing this out to me, as I'd missed it too. The get-set protocol makes it clear, at least, ugly as it is. And note that my rule of "one name per concept" is often in conflict with the noun/verb rule. So, in class GumBall, size(); would retrieve the size of an object and method size(int size); would set a new size. The dilemma is: (a) remember a lot of usages for the same word, vs (b) remember a lot of similar names for a single concept. I normally choose (a), while others would prefer (b). I might use *setSize* in this case, actually.

But, most of the Java conventions are sensible. Do Capitalize the names of classes; use camelCase, not under_scores, for methods and fields. Constant names in ALL UPPERCASE, etc. But a team, since they are sharing code, needs to have a shared convention so they can easily work with each other's contributions. Using a common style is more important that using the *best possible* style. Using a modern IDE that helps to maintain the style is very helpful.

There are two places in *Polymorphism* in which the students give a lesson against using primitives and in favor of using objects in their place. The first is on page 22, where Zahid decides on a design for the model, in which a user will have individual press methods for the numeric keys: *pressThree*. The discussion shows why a simple parameterization using an *int* is a bad design. The programmer has no easy control over what will be passed as an int. However, as the program developed, the students did reach a stage in which parameterization would make sense. We will return to this in a moment, but first, I'd like to consider what this little project might look like in a larger framework, and with a larger team.

It might have been the case that Julie and Zahid were two members of a larger team and other team members were tasked with building a GUI for the calculator. This would be most appropriate in a multi-disciplinary team, as the skills needed for successful user interface design and for successful model building are a bit different, though often held by the same person. But note that the two parts of the team need to coordinate their work and the coordination is precisely at the point of the public methods of the model. Julie and Zahid need no particular knowledge of the GUI, and there may be many distinct user interfaces for a large application, but the other programmers need to know how to invoke the processes of the model. The processes are available through the set of public methods. This is what is called an API:

7

Application Programmer Interface. Java, itself, has a very extensive API, including several packages that most programmers take advantage of, such as java.util. An API is a point of communication and coordination. It permits different groups to proceed relatively independently of one another.

Returning to the choice that Zahid made and the alternatives, note that once they decided to build objects for the numeric keys, it would be possible to provide a method of CalculatorModel so that the GUI programmers could write model.press(three), rather than model.pressThree(). They could enable model.three.press(), in fact, simply by making the NumericKey objects public, rather than private. Since there isn't a fortyTwo key object, the original objection no longer applies. Making the key objects public is not an issue, since their class is private, so an external user can't create the fortyTwo key. Thus, Julie and Zahid maintain appropriate control over the model. But enabling either change would change the API, and doing so might disrupt their colleagues, so such things are normally negotiated in a team, and, one hopes, are well thought out by library designers. Interfaces are good for defining an API.

And, of course, if Julie and Zahid want to enable either of these two API changes they should do so consistently, and then provide actual key objects for equals, clear, etc. Then, the names of the objects become part of the API. This is fine, since they are, in effect, constants. The reader might want to explore using an Enumeration for the NumericKey objects, in fact. Since an Enumeration can have associated methods, this would provide a nice unification of the numeric keys. It would also emphasize that zero..nine is a complete set of numeric keys.

The second instance of a lesson against using primitives, is on page 50 in the discussion about null versus a Null Object. Truth be told, I was always considered a task-master by my students, but I've never actually considered skinning anyone. My most severe admonition is a raised eyebrow, like a big puppy. But the lesson about not using *null* is an important one. Once you introduce null into a program as an object reference you are forever condemned to checking for it or suffering the pain of responding to exceptions. Just Say No! Had they used *null* here, while it would solve the immediate problem, later, on page 59, the test with no operator would have failed with a NullPointerException and they would have work to do. Julie explains this on page 60, in fact. The Null Object pattern lets you replace a primitive, null, with an object over which you have control. Doing the simplest thing that could possibly work doesn't mean you should leave traps like null in your code.

Of course, you must use primitives *somewhere* in most programs. They are the basic *stuff* out of which programs are built. But it is a big advantage to hide them deeply in implementations surrounded by an API that hides their use. You don't see the quarks out of which *you* are built, for example. The NumericKey objects do not have an accessor for their *value*. So the *three key* behaves like a *key*, not like a fountain of 3's. The *value* of a numeric key is used nowhere outside the class itself. Rather than being a *value* provider, it is a *service* provider. Rather than asking the object for some part of its implementation so that a process can be carried out externally using an obtained value, the object performs services on behalf of its clients. True, it is only the *press* service here, but this is a Big Idea. Build classes so that the objects provide services, not values.

Another simple style element in my code is that when a concept is defined in an interface, with several classes implementing that interface, then most variables are declared to have the interface type, not the class type. So, on page 39 you will find:

```
private NumericStrategy accumulate = new AccumulateStrategy();
```

rather than:

```
private AccumulateStrategy accumulate = new AccumulateStrategy();
```

This seems like a small point, but it reminds me that it is a poor design practice to implement an interface with a class that has additional public methods not defined in the interface. Sometimes you need to do this, but you are diverging from implementing abstractions to just implementing *stuff*. In a situation like that, it is better to extend the interface (as NumericKey extends Key) than to just add the methods in the implementing classes. It forces you to think about the abstractions, not just the code. You get errors if you then try to invoke one of the "extra" methods.

The reader of *Polymorphism* will also note the nearly complete absence of comments in the code. I seldom use inline comments, though normally write JavaDoc comments for every non-private feature. Space considerations caused me to omit them. The JavaDoc should simply state the intent of a public method and any required arguments. This lets other programmers depend on just the generated JavaDoc html pages to understand how to use your code, rather than having to actually read the code. You can also, of course, document your intentions about such things as invariants or the immutability of objects, even in private classes and methods.

Some people believe that if you have to comment the code itself, it is probably wrong, or at least too complex. After changes in an iterative development the comments will likely be inconsistent with the code in any case. One of the meta-rules of dealing with a dusty deck (old program) is to ignore, or at least be extremely skeptical of, any comments. Write code in such a way that the code is self-commenting by using clear constructs and intention revealing names. The understandability of your code is almost always more important than any imagined efficiency gains. Efficiency is *only* important when it is. Usually only in a tiny part of any program.

In general it is important and useful to be *explicit* in your coding. Fields and variables should be explicitly initialized, rather than using the compiler-supplied defaults. Imports should be explicit. That is, import java.util.HashSet, rather than java.util.*. Then you know what other components your code depends upon.

And finally, note again that if you are part of a team, it is more important that the team use a common coding style than one considered superior by one of the members. An inconsistency in style will make collaboration very difficult and will be a constant irritant.

You will see more of my code later in this book. The astute reader will notice that I'm not completely consistent. I've warned my students that I'm not perfect, lest they expect it.

Structure

If you examine the UML diagram of the code built in *Polymorphism* (*Polymorphism* pg. 82) you will find that the structure of the code is defined by three interfaces. The calculator model refers directly to these three abstractions and little else. Julie and Zahid did not build a hierarchy of classes, but a trio of abstractions that were implemented in final classes. Rather than define an operator key as a subclass of numeric key, the Key abstraction was extended to a new abstraction: OperatorKey. That abstraction is a valid *specialization* of Key.

There are no methods that are overridden in subclasses. *Override* in this code refers to implementing a method declared in the interface.

The abstract class AllOperators is present just to gather the common *press* method of all the operator keys. And *press* is never overridden in a subclass. No method is overridden anywhere!

This use of inheritance to provide true specialization and nothing else is very powerful. It aids the programmer in thinking about the *abstractions*, not the code. The programmer doesn't need to keep track of different implementations of the same basic thing in different classes. There is always and only one implementation in a hierarchy. Where implementations are different, it is in sibling classes, such as the *operate* methods of Plus and Minus.

On the other hand, the code can be thought of as being built by *composition*, not by inheritance. The CalculatorModel is built up (composed) out of *things*, primarily keys and strategies. I have found this to be a powerful way to think about object-orientation: a facilitator of composition, rather than inheritance.

There was once a book, perhaps it still exists, that gave the prototypical use of inheritance by defining a Cylinder as a subclass of a Circle. The idea was that the circle class already had a radius field, so the Cylinder class simply needed to add a height field. This seems completely backwards to me, a mathematician at heart. If a student learns to program in this way, I think they will never learn to think in terms of abstractions, but only in terms of the lowest level implementations. It is just assembly language with a lot of syntactic sugar. I can think of no advantage of such a hierarchy, either in problem solving or in the efficiency of the resulting generated code. Of course, a cone would then be a circle, also!?!?

It is vital, in my view, to get a firm hold on the idea of specialization in code. If one class, named Extended, extends another, named Base, then it should be possible, conceptually, to think of every object in Extended to be just a Base at heart. It isn't possible to think of a Cylinder as a Circle, so that isn't specialization and so Cylinder extends Circle is just wrong. Make your code reflect the concepts in the problem space. </rant>

Packages in Java are also about structure. If you search online for the reason for Java packages, you get mostly technical discussions. I view it differently. To me, a package defines the *boundary* of the work of a single team. Within that boundary team members share code widely and so don't worry excessively about encapsulation. This assumes the team is small, of course. Encapsulation isn't to "protect" some code from other code. It is to permit a programmer to set boundaries that other *programmers* can't cross, so that there can be stability within the boundary. Information hiding isn't about hiding code from other code, but from other programmers. Think in terms of the team's *responsibility boundary*. If anyone in a large team can change anything – chaos. So, a package defines an API for *other* programmers. Sometimes, however, certain coding signals, like *protected*, can serve to warn or suggest to your team mates that some things should be preserved. But make sure you understand the meaning of *protected*. It is, and should be, seldom used other than in base libraries since it opens visibility outside the package and implies subclassing. In a large project a small team might be responsible for several packages of course.

In *Polymorphism*, it was suggested that the student collect the two display fields into a single object. That has interesting possibilities, especially when it is built with a top-level class, fully encapsulated. Building such a class and integrating it into Julie and Zahid's code can also show a more traditional view of object-orientation, as well as introduce some other high level ideas. The Display class can be a true abstraction. It will encapsulate two values, but it isn't entirely obvious that it does. The class should perform services for the calculator, not just provide values. It should be possible to move much of the arithmetic into this object. It should have a minimum of accessors and its mutators should not be obviously just setters of fields. Below is one way to do this: Spoiler Alert.

For a reason that I'll only reveal later, I'll start with an interface defining my desired protocol.

```
package juliezahid.calculator;

public interface Display {

    public abstract int current();

    public abstract void clear();

    public abstract void shift();

    public abstract void accumulate(int value);

    public abstract void apply(Operation operation)
            throws ArithmeticException;
}
```

This protocol will be modified later, but will do for now. The last method may seem strange and we delay the explanation for a page or so. Ordinarily, defining this as an interface makes little sense, as there is only one display object in a calculator. However, in this case we will actually be trying to build something more generally useful: something that might be used in a different sort of calculator. There might even be different sorts of displays. An auditory display for the blind would be useful, for example.

The SimpleDisplay class starts out like this, as a top-level class within the same package:

```
package juliezahid.calculator;

public class SimpleDisplay implements Display{
    private int current = 0;
    private int previous = 0;

    public int current(){
        return current;
    }

    public void clear(){
        current = 0;
    }
    ...
```

The *current* field is the current display value and we need an accessor for it, say for any eventual GUI that we build. We also know from one of the stories that we need to be able to clear the current display.

Another useful method is *shift*: which shifts the current display into the previous field to save it.

```
public void shift(){
    previous = current;
}
```

Note that both *shift* and *clear* are mutators, as they change the state of the display object and any computation using it.

We also include the accumulation process (a service) in the display.

```
public void accumulate(int value){
    current = 10 * current + value;
}
```

Note that we don't include a mutator for the *current* field, since, assuming a Display object is named *display*, a client can write:

```
display.clear();
display.accumulate(5);
```

to set 5 into the display as the current value.

As an exercise, think about what you would do to build a display for a base-8 calculator, rather than the normal base-10. If you add a constructor, you could make it work for any base.

So far, what we have here is pretty clean. A Display object mostly provides services, such as clear and accumulate. But it isn't powerful enough to serve in the CalculatorModel yet, since we don't have a way to perform the arithmetic operations. Note, in particular that there is no accessor for the *previous* field. We would like all of those operations to be performed as services, also, without revealing the fact that there are really two fields. Of course, the *shift* method gives a hint, but *shift* can be described in terms of *operands* for the calculator, rather than *fields* for the display.

One way to handle this would be to give the Display a set of methods, one per operation. But that would mean that to add a new operation, we need to modify the class (and its interface). Let's see if we can get away with adding a single method that will handle all of the anticipated binary operations: plus, minus, etc.

Suppose that we first provide an abstraction of a binary operation like this; a top-level interface:

```
package juliezahid.calculator;

public interface Operation {
    public int apply(int first, int second);
}
```

This is the Operation that was mentioned in our mysterious last method of the Display interface. The *apply* method of an adding object that implements the Operation interface would return the sum of the two arguments, *first* and *second*.

Next, let's add the remaining method to the SimpleDisplay class:

```
public void apply(Operation operation)
        throws ArithmeticException{
    current = operation.apply(current, previous);
}
```

The *apply* method of a SimpleDisplay uses the Operation provided as a parameter by, in turn, *applying* it to *current* and *previous*, giving a new *current*. We need to be able to signal errors from such operations, so we advertise that apply might throw an ArithmeticException, as indeed it should if we try to divide by zero in an operation. And note my *single name for a single concept: apply.*

We can then have a set of top-level classes, each in their own file, which implement the Operation interface. In effect, the objects defined by these classes act just as if they were functions. For example:

```
package juliezahid.calculator;
public class Subtracter implements Operation{

    @Override
    public int apply(int first, int second) {
        return second - first;
    }
}
```

Objects like these are very simple, stateless, and immutable. To add a new binary operation, we define a new class, leaving everything else unchanged. The CalculatorModel would then be able to take advantage of the new operation with no changes to the display's class. So, the display is well encapsulated and polymorphic.

With this infrastructure, the Minus (inner) class of the CalculatorModel becomes:

```
private final class Minus extends AllOperators { // Singleton
    private Operation subtract = new Subtracter();
    @Override
    public final void operate() {
        display.apply(subtract);
        resetState();
    }
}
```

In the above, we assume that the CalculatorModel has a field named *display* of class SimpleDisplay as above.

All of the other operations of CalculatorModel can be re-written in terms of the Display interface and simple classes like the Subtracter. The result will pass all of the original tests without changing the tests at all. Note that, now, the Display provides services for the arithmetic operations using the Operation objects.

We can even add the sign change operation using this mechanism:

```
package juliezahid.calculator;

public class SignChanger implements Operation {

    @Override
    public int apply(int first, int second) {
        return -first;
    }

}
```

It just ignores the second operand.

So, the *apply* method of an Operation is very general and therefore makes the Display quite general. However, the accumulate method now stand out as being very special. It is easy to generalize this operation by adding an additional method to the Display interface that will cover this case and many more, as well. The new method will also be called *apply* (there I go again):

```
public abstract void apply(Operation operation, int value)
        throws ArithmeticException;
```

The only difference is that it supplies an additional parameter that can be used in some way.

We implement this method in the SimpleDisplay class as follows.

```
public void apply(Operation operation, int value)
        throws ArithmeticException {
    current = operation.apply(current, value);
}
```

Note that it uses the *apply* method of the Operation in a very different way, ignoring the *previous* field of the calculator.

In particular. Accumulate can be realized as an application of this new *apply* method by using the following Operation.

```
package juliezahid.calculator;

public class Accumulator implements Operation {

    @Override
    public int apply(int first, int second) {
        return first * 10 + second;
    }

}
```

With the changes, the final version of our Display interface looks like this:

```
package juliezahid.calculator;

public interface Display {
```

```
        public abstract int current();

        public abstract void clear();

        public abstract void shift();

        public abstract void apply(Operation operation);
                throws ArithmeticException;

        public abstract void apply(Operation operation, int value)
                throws ArithmeticException;
}
```

I will leave it as an exercise to the reader to modify the CalculatorModel to use a Display instead of the *display* and *oldDisplay* fields in the original version. The tests should remain unchanged. Only the CalculatorModel is affected. This is a major refactoring, of course.

The code for the Display and associated interfaces and classes may be downloaded from the following location. Other software discussed in this book can be found there also. However, only the simplest versions of the programs are available as I don't want to interfere with your fun. Most can be extended and modified.

http://csis.pace.edu/~bergin/polymorphismCompanionBook/downloads.html

What makes the Display interface especially interesting is that we can supply an alternative implementation of it that will be useful here in more than one way, but it will also permit us to build a different sort of calculator.

We will call the new class RPNDisplay for a reason that will become clear later. The most important difference in the new class is that it uses a Java Stack in place of the display fields. This means that we aren't limited to just two display fields, or any fixed number. We will, however, impose an *invariant* on our stack. We will guarantee that it always has at least two elements. This is so that our binary operations will always succeed, other than division by zero. If an operation would otherwise leave a stack with fewer than 2 elements, zeros are supplied for the additional values. In effect, this means that we have an infinite stack that is "zeros all the way down."

The RPNDisplay starts out like this:

```
package juliezahid.calculator;
import java.util.Stack;

/**
 *      Invariant: Always contains at least two elements
 */
public class RPNDisplay implements Display {
    private Stack<Integer> stack = new Stack<Integer>();

    public RPNDisplay(){
        stack.push(0);
        stack.push(0);
    }

    @Override
    public int current() {
        return stack.peek();
    }

    @Override
    public void clear() {
        stack.pop();
        stack.push(0);
    }

    @Override
    public void shift() {
        stack.push(stack.peek());
    }
}
```

Note that clear doesn't clear the entire stack, but only puts zero into the top element. The remaining elements are unaffected. Also, shift acts a bit differently in this version of a display, since the old second element, *previous* of the earlier version, isn't overwritten, but just pushed farther down the stack, as are other elements if present. But, in general, with that understanding, the top of the stack is like the earlier *current* and the second element is like *previous*.

The basic idea for binary operators in this display is that we will pop two elements off the stack, apply the operator to those values, and then push the result back on to the stack. But since two have been removed, but one put back, we need to also guarantee our invariant.

```java
@Override
public void apply(Operation operation)
        throws ArithmeticException {
    int top = stack.pop();
    int previous = stack.pop();
    if(stack.isEmpty()){
        stack.push(0);
    }
    stack.push(operation.apply(top, previous));
}
```

Here again is a small difference between the RPNDisplay and the earlier version. In the SimpleDisplay class, after a binary operation, the previous operand was left unchanged. Here, however, it has been removed (and possibly replaced by zero). However, if we replace the stack.pop() with stack.peek() in setting the *previous* local variable above, we would get behavior like that of SimpleDisplay. Note the IF statement above. Trying to make this polymorphic is most likely a mistake, so won't be attempted. There are, however, one or two ways to extend the Stack class so that guaranteeing that we always have a second operand would be automatic. The cleanest version of this is to define a stack class that is given a default value in its constructor. Then, when you attempt to pop an empty stack you get the default value instead of an exception being thrown. But, most likely, that would just move the IF statement, not remove it.

The version of *apply* that handles unary operators, operating on the top of the stack, looks like this:

```
@Override
    public void apply(Operation operation, int value)
            throws ArithmeticException {
        stack.push(operation.apply(stack.pop(), value));
    }
```

That completes the RPNDisplay class. It is interesting to note, that if we replace the SimpleDisplay object in CalculatorModel with an RPNDisplay object, we will still pass all of the original tests. That isn't to say that the two calculators behave identically. We have noted above that they do not, but both pass all of the tests driven by the stories without otherwise changing the CalculatorModel class.

However, this new sort of display gives us a few new opportunities. Recall that the precedence of operators was explicitly removed from consideration in the Calculator stories. Suppose that the customer desires to bring it back. Currently a sequence of key presses like 5 + 3 * 2 = produces 16. The operators are evaluated strictly left to right. However, with precedence, it would produce 11, since the multiplication needs to be performed before the addition.

In order to implement precedence, the program needs to do two things. One is to remember an earlier operator that has had its operation delayed. The other is to remember an operand for that operator. The stack-based display makes the second requirement automatic. At the point at which the multiplication is done in the above example, the stack has 2, 3, and 5, in that order from the top. So, when the multiplication is finished the stack will have 6, then 5, and the addition will produce 11.

However, the program still needs to remember earlier operators as well. Note that we only have two levels of precedence with the operators so far suggested in the stories. If there were many, it might be advantageous to define an additional stack of operators.

Here, however, there is a much simpler solution. Suppose that we simply have a *currentHighOperator* and a *currentLowOperator* in CalculatorModel, rather than just the *currentOperator*. Both are initially set to *noOperator*. When a multiplication is indicated, *currentHighOperator* becomes that operator. Then, when one of the low operators is about to *operate*, we send *operate* to the *currentHighOperator* first. What makes this possible is that there will only be one delayed operator here (with two levels of precedence), since operations at the same level are executed in the order of the button presses. We leave the details to the reader. There is a story about this in a future section.

But it is also possible to use the RPNDisplay to build a calculator similar to those produced by Hewlett-Packard, such as the HP 15C. Those calculators, called Reverse Polish Notation calculators, ask the user to enter both operands of a binary operation into the calculator before indicating which operation is to be applied to them. The two operands need to be separated by another key press, so that the calculator doesn't just accumulate across the two operands. That key is typically called *Enter* or *Push*, and the calculator internally uses a stack to hold operands. RPN is also called postfix notation. The original Polish Notation, or prefix notation, was created by Jan Łukasiewicz, but no one, seemingly, wanted to try to remember how to spell his name. In prefix notation, the operator comes before its two operands. We will provide stories for the creation of a simple RPN calculator in a future section. Note, however, that many of the early Hewlett-Packard calculators have a stack of limited depth, often just four items. We have no such limit here. If that behavior is explicitly required you can use a finite stack, of course.

The advantage of RPN is that you don't need parentheses to indicate precedence when you want to override the normal rules. In a fancy algebraic calculator there are usually special keys to parenthesize a complex expression. You can see this on page 2 of *Polymorphism*.

Better Living Through Programming

Stories, Additional Stories, Alternate Stories

An agile software project proceeds something like this. The sponsor of a software system starts with an idea and explores it as needed, usually on the business side of an organization, hopefully with end-users of the eventual product. He or she then gathers a team together consisting of developers, testers, and other specialists. This initial team, with the sponsor or a delegate taking the role of customer then brainstorms the project for a few days, developing the overall concept so that everyone has a fairly good idea of the direction to be followed. The customer, with guidance of the developers, starts to write stories for the project. The team attempts to get the most important features in the story list and also an initial set of stories that, when built, will give an end-to-end version of the product, though with many features omitted. An overall design and architecture need not be done, but might be, depending on the critical nature of the application and how tightly it must integrate with other systems. If an architecture is developed it is understood that it could change, so it doesn't need to be as complete as might be the case if the project were less agile.

We are now in the second or third week of the project and little money has been spent. The customer selects a subset of the stories and the developers estimate how long it will take to build each one. If an individual story is so large as to take the team more than a couple of weeks (or preferably, days) to complete and test, the story is split. Then the customer selects, from among the estimated stories, enough, but not too much, to represent two weeks of work and the developers start to build just those stories as if it were the complete project. Everything is tested as it is built and integrated into a whole, though incomplete, application. Precisely at the end of two weeks development stops, whether done or not, and the results are presented to the customer. Along the way, the customer has verified each story when the developers believe it to be done. He or she is the final and only arbiter of the meaning of *done*. These two weeks have been called an iteration, or a sprint. For some projects an iteration lasts a month, but still, fixed in length.

The customer then has a number of options, including canceling the project. But, more likely the customer is happy with some things and unhappy with others. To resolve any unhappiness, the customer simply writes additional stories, which may require rework of what has been done. After all, what the customer wanted a few weeks ago might not be wanted now. This is sometimes true because seeing the application lets him or her rethink what they really want, and it is sometimes true that the need has simply changed. These new stories are estimated in the usual way, the customer chooses stories for the next two weeks and the process repeats until the project is done or abandoned. The smart customer will schedule high value stories early in the process. Thus the value of the next story declines while the cost of integrating it may rise. When the cost and value curves cross, it is time to declare the project done. Of course, changing needs may change the value curve.

Within an iteration the developers are in control of the order in which to build the stories, and the means and methodologies. The customer cannot change the order of work within an iteration, but has complete control between iterations. The customer, however, is the one to judge that a story is complete.

Many teams use Pair Programming and other useful team practices to see that the iteration is successful. An iteration ends at a certain date and time and is never extended. There is an extensive literature of several variations of this, including XP and Scrum. Most teams employ a *Coach* o r *Scrum Master* to keep them performing the tasks required by the process.

Within the classroom, some of these practices have been found to be helpful. As should be obvious, I like Pair Programming and Story Driven Development. An implication of this, however, is that the students should, ideally, deliver things periodically rather than all at once, and the professor/customer should give them redirection on how to proceed to the next iteration. Thus, stories may change. They may change before an iteration begins, or even after the iteration is complete and they were thought done. It doesn't mean someone has failed, but only that the needs are seen to be different now than previously. This requires rework, of course.

Changing a story is also a good way to introduce students to the issues in dealing with changes to an existing code base: the *dusty deck* problem. This is named for the days in which Fortran and Cobol programs were represented by a deck of 80 column IBM cards, one card per statement. An old program had been sitting on a shelf, somewhere and became a dusty deck. But then it needed updating. Oh My. The big problem with a dusty deck is that you don't understand what it does and any documentation is probably inconsistent with the program itself. In order to proceed with an update, you should form hypotheses about the behavior and test them. Since the program itself is unlikely to have a test suite to go with it, it is productive to start to develop a suite to capture your hypotheses. When you make changes, the test can help you along.

Before tackling a few new and modified stories for the calculator, I suggest you explore a few things that were not covered in the original stories. This is probably because the customer just didn't think to say anything about them. If any of the developers had done so it would have been good to bring them to the attention of the customer. What, for example, does CalculatorModel do in a situation like 5 + 3 + =? Or, how does it respond to + 5 =? Are these sensible. Note that the application does *something*, even if it wasn't planned. This is one of the reasons that virus code is enabled in many applications. Someone didn't think about a possible input sequence before the black hats did.

Here are a few additional stories and modifications to existing stories. You can consider each to be an independent request to modify the code produced by the end of *Polymorphism*. The first is a change to story 6. Likewise, 9a is a modification of Story 9, etc.

6a. Multiple Equals: Pressing = a second time *will* repeat the current operation. Display is updated. Pressing = when there is no outstanding operation will be ignored.

e.g. 5 + 3 = = should result in 11.

e.g. 5 − 3 = = gives -1.

9a. Clear Entry: Give the calculator a *ClearEntry* key that will clear the current operand, but leave outstanding operations in place. The display should show 0. Immediately pressing *ClearEntry* a second time will clear the calculation completely, as *Clear* does. Then drop the *clear* button.

13. Missing Second Operand: Pressing = immediately after pressing an operator key will be ignored. e.g. 5 + = ignores the =. The display shows 5.

Or:

13a. Missing Second Operand: Pressing = immediately after pressing an operator key is an error. A GUI would display "Error".

Story 13a requires something like a new exception.

14. Precedence: Multiplication and division take precedence over addition and subtraction. 5 + 3 * 2 = should result in 11.

Story 14 will probably require changing the *display* structure to a stack of some sort. If the two display fields haven't already been unified in a single object, it would be a good time to do so. Note the interaction with Story 6a. Propose a resolution.

15. Change Sign: Give the calculator a Change Sign key that changes the sign of the display.

Another concept sometimes seen in Agile Projects is a Developer Story. This is usually a way to find time to do a major refactoring. It is estimated and scheduled in the usual way, though it may take some negotiation with the customer to get it into an iteration. For example:

> 16. Enumeration: Refactor the application so that numeric keys are represented by an Enumeration.

The next one requires that the test file be refactored as well, since it calls for a change in the API.

> 17. Key Objects: Give the application Key objects for all keys. The key objects should be public, enabling an alternate API, such as
>
> model.press(three); or model.three.press();
>
> Remove the other press methods from the API.

And of course:

> 18. GUI: Give the application a Graphical User Interface (View). The display is at the top, the operator keys at the right, and numeric keys at the left

I usually implement such stories, especially those requiring changes, by *versioning* my project. Make a copy of the project and modify that instead of the original.

Sorry, haiku not
maybe close, abstract a bit
fun to play with still

Test, Test, Testing

In traditional waterfall development, testing comes late; too late to affect the quality of the product. Too often it just tells you that you are about to deploy junk. One of the key insights that led to Extreme Programming was that if something was a good idea, as testing is, then you should do it all the time. Turn the knob to 10. This led to Test First Development, in which tests do help maintain quality. Early tests are good. Earlier tests are better. Make the testing come before the development. QED. The tests are tied to the stories and capture a shared understanding between customer and developer about the needs. *All* the knobs to 10 is extreme.

In the educational environment testing can also be a vital adjunct to learning. The professor can provide tests initially. She can develop some early tests in a demonstration session, for example. The tests make it specific what must be done, and since they are executable there is no ambiguity about when the student has succeeded. Moreover, the tests, if well designed, can guide the student into how to solve a particular problem. On page 69 of *Polymorphism*, Julie gets a key idea from looking at the test.

And of course you need the *correct* tests. Unit test written by the developers, say students, test only the developer's understanding of the requirements. The customer/owner may have a different idea. When these are not in sync, bad things happen as did occur with Julie and Zahid. Most of the time, the sponsor of a story won't be a technical genius and won't be able to develop tests him or herself. There is a separate testing structure used in Agile Software Development in which tests are written using separate tools that do capture the intent of the customer. One of these tools, FIT, uses spreadsheets. It also has a web interface, http://fitnesse.org. But an instructor teaching programming can certainly use JUnit to provide tests as an adjunct to student-written tests. The negative aspect of this is that the tests will give names to methods of the application tested. If the professor provides the tests, he or she is actually defining the API of the code that the students build. This may be desirable or not, depending on the level of sophistication of the students. Early on, it is likely a good thing, and the students will be more able to handle their own test development as they progress. Later on, you may be able to check student-written tests, rather than providing them yourself. You can also use class time, or the class list, to develop tests.

However, note that there is no code in the application itself to support testing. Private methods remain private. Don't provide return values from methods unless the application itself requires them. There are no accessor methods introduced to support testing, etc. The test suite stands completely apart from the application. This is an important concept. Among other things it means that an error in the test suite can't crash the application, though it could, of course, lead you to build the wrong thing.

The other key idea is that unit tests are a form of *regression* testing. They are executable and are executed whenever a change is committed to the application itself. It is very difficult to build buggy code if your tests are complete and correct. They are also written and executed early enough that they cause you to fix any problems as they occur. This, of course, is when they are fresh in your mind. So you don't need to reconstruct thought processes as would occur if a test is only run for the first time at the end of development. Also, the test size/granularity is small. A failed test requires a small fix, not a large one, in most cases.

Test First is a bit harder for GUI applications. It isn't impossible, but is a bit awkward, often depending on a separate scripting language that will exercise a graphical interface. Some tools require that you put some helper code into the application, which is problematic, as I've suggested above. This is another good reason for carefully splitting the application into Model and Views.

A later project here will show how you can use JUnit to test an interactive application in which user input normally comes from a keyboard.

Testing. Hitting 11 on the 1 to 10 scale!

In Praise of Études

Via Wikipedia:

> An étude (/ 'eɪtjuːd/; French pronunciation: [e'tyd], a French word meaning study) is an instrumental musical composition, usually short, of considerable difficulty, and designed to provide practice material for perfecting a particular musical skill.

It is easy to argue that most programming assignments given to students are études. But it is useful for a professor to think specifically about developing them as such. While there is nothing in the above definition that implies that musical études are beautiful music, often they are, and often they are performed for their beauty, not just their difficulty. But the difficulty forces the performer to expand his or her skill in ways that are hard to achieve otherwise. But only if mastered – practiced repeatedly.

The Polymorphism Étude is easy to translate to other important skills; the Recursion Étude, for example. Of course, it implies that it is focused on a *desirable* skill. One exercise that was useful, back in the days in which Fortran ruled, was to try to write a single program that would generate every compiler diagnostic error. It gave insight into why programs go wrong. Another might be to write a program that uses every Java built-in statement and expression type at least once, yet does something useful. Another might exercise some Java library in an interesting way. These probably aren't real études, as they lack the repeatability element.

Related to the concept of an étude, is that of *creativity under constraint*. Some craftspeople who make fine furniture, for example, do so without any power tools. They put a constraint on their tool set. Others make only one sort of thing, say cabinets. They put a constraint on their output forms. What can you accomplish if you constrain some aspect of what you do? What can you build without IF statements? What sort of a poem can you write if you restrict yourself to only one form? Does it mean that the result is necessarily less beautiful or useful than it would have been if you used a richer toolset? Can practicing one form help with others?

The Iliad, a story that takes place near the end of the Trojan Wars, was composed entirely in dactylic hexameter, a very restrictive form. It contains more than fifteen thousand lines. It is believed to have been recited orally for hundreds of years before being captured in writing. A modern translator normally wants to keep the form as well as the story. It is difficult to do so, but the Iliad, even in translation, is beautiful.

In some ways it is easier to create under constraint than otherwise. This seems backwards, but is often true. If you are tasked with writing a poem, you often don't know where to start. The task seems hard. There are too many options. But if you are asked to write haiku, your task is much narrower. Your form and subject matter are both constrained. The task seems easier, than when you had more options. Indeed, the form of the Iliad is said to have aided both the original composition and the memorization by its reciters.

But the essence of a true étude, is that it be practiced. It is not just to be done once or a few times and forgotten. Repetition is the key. I've practiced T'ai Chi Ch'uan since 2004. I do a Yang Style Long Form. The form has about a hundred moves and never changes. It is practiced several times a week, preferably daily. Preferably several times a day. It is, essentially, an étude. The more you practice the better you become, the more you understand self-defense, the better control you have over your body, and the healthier you get. But one seeks improvement not perfection, which is likely not attainable.

Once you practice an étude often enough, it can become second nature. In the case of polymorphism, you start to see the opportunities to employ it as readily as you see the "need" for an IF statement. At that point you are ready to make an informed judgement about the relative desirability of each possible solution.

Play it again, Sam.

Yet Another Calculator

Earlier we developed a Display interface along with an RPNDisplay. Here we provide some guidance in the development of an RPNCalculatorModel. I suggest that you and a partner implement the following stories using Test Driven Development. The result should be an RPN calculator. If you use the RPNDisplay developed above, the work is much simpler than the algebraic calculator that Julie and Zahid built in *Polymorphism*. An RPN calculator doesn't have an *equals* key. Instead, it has a key labelled *Enter* or *Push*. Such calculators are elegant in their simplicity.

First, let's look at how such a calculator operates. Instead of a sequence such as 5 + 3 = to perform an addition, the sequence of key presses now will be 5 push 3 +. The operation is applied immediately on seeing the operator and the two operands are already available. Precedence is handled by the user, rather than being built in. So 5 push 3 + 2 × gives 16, since the addition is performed first. But 5 push 3 push 2 × + gives 11, since the 3 and 2 are multiplied, giving 6 on the stack, which is then added to the 5. Note that the stack is part of the mental model of the user of such a calculator. So the following stories really are relevant to a user.

The first few stories are identical to those of the original calculator. When I built this I found the structure much simpler. I never felt that I needed to build numeric key objects, for example. Of course, if you and your partner would rather have an API that doesn't include methods such as pressThree, then your program will be different than mine.

> 1. Zero Display: Create a calculator that will give you its display. A new calculator should have a display of 0.

Since you already have the RPNDisplay class, start with that as the implementation of the display. But write a test for the story first.

2. Single Numeric Key: Give the calculator keys like 5 and 3. When you hit a single key the value of the key should "show" in the display.

3. Accumulate: If you press a sequence of number keys, the results should accumulate in the display.

Recall that the RPNDisplay already "knows" how to accumulate if you just apply an Accumulator object.

4. Push. Give the calculator a *push* key that will push the current display onto a stack and allow the entry of another operand. The display is unchanged.

This is the first new story. Strategies like the ResetStrategy are probably still useful in this version.

5. Operator Key: Give the calculator a + key that adds the results of two operands. The operation is applied to the two top stack elements, with the result replacing them on the stack and in the display. Other operator keys will be added later (-, *, /). Note: Assure the stack always has at least two elements. The key sequence for a simple addition is something like 5 push 3 +, yielding 8. Also, the sequence 5 push + should yield 10.

Operator keys are applied immediately, unlike the algebraic calculator in which the operation is delayed, waiting for the second argument.

Again, recall that the Display "knows" how to perform binary operations using Operation objects.

6. Minus Key: Implement a minus key to be sure you have the correct associativity. The latest operand is subtracted from the previous one.

55 push 30 - yields 25.

7. Multiple Calculations: After completing a computation it should be possible to carry out another computation immediately. For example 5 push 3 + 5 push 5 + should yield 10.

What happens if you push minus at the end of the sequence suggested in Story 7? Is that the most desirable outcome? If so, do you want to capture it in a Story and one or more tests?

8. Clear All: Give the calculator a Clear key that will clear any outstanding operations, just as if it were turned off then on again. The display is 0.

9. Clear Entry: Give the calculator a ClearEntry key that will pop the top element from the stack. The display will show the item previously just below the top. Other items are moved up.

Don't neglect the invariant.

10. Multiple Operators: An expression may have multiple operators, not just one. For example, 53 push 3 + 5 + should give 61. Note that 53 push 3 push 5 + + has the same effect.

11. Complete Key Set: Add the rest of the keys, numeric and operator. The division operator does integer division: 5/3 gives 1. Dividing by zero should throw a run time exception. Alternatively return the minimum integer value.

12. Change Sign. Give the calculator a key that will change the sign of the display

13. Swap. Give the calculator a key that will swap the top two elements on the stack.

There are other possibilities that you might explore. The calculator could compute in decimals, rather than integers. It can even use Java's BigInteger, a representation of all of the integers, rather than a subset. BigDecimal is another possibility. You could explore RPN calculators online. What additional keys might be added to your calculator. Which of those are easy, and which more difficult?

An HP calculator actually retains its state when shut off. You might think about how to realize that in a software calculator. The Animal Game, presented later, will give some ideas about that. The display is easy to save. Saving strategies might require a bit more ingenuity. I would avoid the Java Serializable mechanism, however, in favor of a text based solution. If you do this, then Story 8, Clear All, needs to be rephrased.

And note that there is information given in these stories that goes beyond what you normally get from a non-technical customer. Story 5, for example, gives more direction than is usual. In some cases, this sort of direction should be ignored. It is the developer who should know *how* to do it.

Yet Another Project

The project described here is due to Alistair Cockburn. He created it as a design exercise, though here we will treat it as one for program development. It admits a truly elegant solution. We present a set of stories for its development as a program. The rest is up to you. You should use Test First Development, of course.

The idea is to build the model for the simulation of a Coffee Machine. The machine can dispense a variety of products created from a variety of ingredients. It takes money and dispenses product, or error messages. In reality, all this program will do is dispense *messages* about its behavior. The messages might be thought of as the log of the actions of a real machine. For example:

After a CoffeeMachine was created and initialized, some money was inserted and a product chosen. Following is the output.

```
40 cents inserted.
BlackCoffee chosen.
Dispensing: Cup
Dispensing: Coffee
Dispensing: Water
BlackCoffee dispensed.
Returning: 5 cents.
```

A failed transaction might look like the following, or be a bit more elaborate, perhaps explaining the reason for failure:

```
25 cents inserted.
BlackCoffee chosen.
BlackCoffee transaction failed.
Coin Return pressed.
Returning: 25 cents.
```

We will give seventeen stories altogether. The first six should be built together as an iteration, without consideration of any other stories. Ideally, students should not even see the rest of the stories prior to building the first six. The stories are written as if it is a physical machine, but "having a button" (Story 5) simply means that the functionality is there and it could be connected to a button in a GUI or a physical machine.

> 1. Coffee: Coffee Machine sells coffee for $.35

> 2. Take Change: It takes only coins/change -- no bills/notes.

> 3. Make Change: It returns change when possible. Change return is automatic after a successful transaction.

> 4. Products: Coffee can be black, with creamer, with sugar, or with both creamer and sugar.

> 5. Look and Feel: It has a button for each product plus coin return.

After inserting money, the customer might press coin return, rather than selecting a product, to cancel the transaction.

> 6. Safety: It won't dispense if it doesn't have sufficient ingredients:
>
> cup, water, coffee, milk powder, sugar, money

The project owner notes that water must be the last ingredient dispensed. Assume that the dispensers know how to dispense a single unit of their ingredient. Water is unlimited as the machine is connected to a water line. The others are limited resources.

If a customer selects a product when insufficient money has been inserted, nothing happens. More money may be inserted or the customer may press the coin return to cancel.

The elegant solution mentioned above has the property that while it is appropriate for the above six stories, and is not over-built, it needs no essential structural changes to add the rest of the stories, with the possible exception of the last. My core implementation has five classes, two of which are enumerations (enum). The enumeration objects have a number of methods. There are some IF statements, but the program isn't just a naïve SWITCH to handle the options. I need one more class to complete the stories.

The reader is encouraged to build a program implementing these six stories before reading the additional stories, which appear later in the book. Pair up and get busy. Don't forget your tests.

The stories above adhere closely to Alistair's originals.

If you teach object-oriented design, this exercise is also very valuable. The output, in that case, is something like a UML model rather than a program. I've used this several times in that way. Student models are projected on a screen to the class and discussed. It is useful to see a lot of designs, even bad ones, to help you learn the elements of a good design.

"Good design comes from experience. Experience comes from bad design." Fred Brooks.

The Polymorphism Challenge

In *Polymorphism*, I made the claim that it is almost always possible to program without IF and SWITCH statements. It isn't always desirable, of course, but as a skill builder, études, such as the Polymorphism Étude, are very important. Ask any musician. In this section I'd like to demonstrate how a simple test in an IF can be transformed into polymorphic code. But be warned, the code that will result is not an improvement over the original. In nearly every case you would be foolish to actually deploy this solution, though I can think of one. I'm also not going to promise that there won't be any IF or SWITCH statements *anywhere* in the program. I'll use library code here that I'm pretty sure was not built polymorphically. But I will find a solution in which I don't need to add any more.

In *Polymorphism*, I focused on the situation in which the state of a computation needed to be not only tested, but the state change made semi-permanent. So, we captured the change in a Strategy object that could be exercised later. But, of course, it isn't always necessary to do that, and some decisions are very ephemeral. Here, I'll focus on that situation. Suppose you have an IF statement with some simple test condition, perhaps the comparison of two int values. Suppose further that the IF and ELSE clauses are long and complicated. Perhaps:

```
if(a < b){

    ...
    // big mess o' code
    ...

} else {

    ...
    // another big mess o' code
    ...

}
```

The first factorization that a sensible programmer would make, of course, is to write helper methods for the long code sections. We assume that these methods might return some value, or might change the state of the object. I'll use a form here, in which it will be easy to test that we get the transformation correct. Normally that is not the right way to proceed, but this is just an exercise. Something like this:

```java
private boolean bigMessFirst(){
    // suppose lots of code here resulting in:
    return true;
}

private boolean bigMessSecond(){
    // suppose lots of code here resulting in:
    return false;
}

public boolean secondVersion(int a, int b){
    if(a < b){
        return bigMessFirst();
    }
    return bigMessSecond();
}
```

That transformation is perfectly logical and would be applied by most programmers to avoid having the IF statement spread over many pages of code. Note that our big messes of code may either require access to non-local variables or, possibly extensive, parameterization. That doesn't change the applicability here, but might make it even messier to do. And note that the *return* within the IF statement means we don't need an ELSE here.

The following transformations are questionable for use in practice, but useful as an étude.

The next step is to move the big messes into individual objects, rather than just as private methods. The solution here is very general, provided that the classes we write are Inner classes at the same level as the code above. If the functions are actually mutators of the containing object it would be difficult to make these classes "top-level".

First we need an interface. This can be a separate file (i.e. top-level) in the same package. We shall call it State, and it would be possible for the application to hold a current reference to such an object for a semi-permanent change, though we won't need to do that here.

```
private interface State{
    public boolean evaluate();
}
```

Of course, if we required parameterization above, we will here also.

Next, we shall implement this twice, with inner classes, so that we separate the two "big mess" code blocks into separate objects. The names of the classes are abstract, since we haven't given a larger "problem" context in which to frame the names.

```
private class StateFirst implements State{
    public boolean evaluate(){
        return bigMessFirst();
    }
}

private class StateSecond implements State{
    public boolean evaluate(){
        return bigMessSecond();
    }
}
```

Of course, we could expand the two functions here, or just keep them as is. The effect is the same. But if I *evaluate* an object of the first class, I get the first big mess o' code executed. Again, note that the return type of boolean isn't essential, but makes testing easy. Next we need an object from each of these classes:

```java
private State trueState = new StateFirst();
private State falseState = new StateSecond();
```

We can use these as follows. Our original simple IF statement, now wrapped in a method, looks like this after transformation. It has also been parametrized for testing purposes.

```java
public boolean thirdVersion(int a, int b) {
    if(a < b){
        return trueState.evaluate();
    }
    return falseState.evaluate();
}
```

This is a very dubious transformation, of course. Why would you do that? Note that it isn't polymorphic yet and is just plain more complex than the original. Well, maybe we can learn something about the relationship between polymorphic and ad hoc code. But that is the end of our second transformation. On to the third. It won't get prettier, I'm afraid.

Note that the "decision space" for our IF statement is infinite (logically, and very large in any case). It is based on values of both *a* and *b*. We can simplify it a bit by basing the decision on b-a instead, as in if(0 < b-a){... But the space is still just as large. The next step, however, is to reduce the space to only two values, using a mapping function. This one will map the "true" space of our original test expression into the value 1 and the "false" space into value 0. The correct function is as follows, but it needs a lot of testing to assure it – or solid analysis. Preferably both.

What it does, in effect, is to collapse the entire right half of the number line into value 1 and the left half into value 0.

```
public int map(int a, int b){
    int result = Math.min(1, b-a);
    result = Math.max(result, 0);
    return result;
}
```

You can test that if a < b this yields 1, otherwise 0. In particular, if they are equal you get 0. So, if a < b is true, you get 1, otherwise 0.

And yes, I realize that the way Math.max and Math.min are implemented almost certainly use simple tests, so, in effect, all I'm doing here is hiding the tests.

The next element of our transformation is a HashMap from java.util. I'll need to initialize the map as well with the values we created in the previous version.

```
private HashMap<Integer, State> theMap =
        new HashMap<Integer, State>();

private void setUp(){
    theMap.put(0, falseState);
    theMap.put(1, trueState);
}
```

And at last, we can see the fully polymorphic version of our original:

```
public boolean versionFour(int a, int b) {
    setUp();
    return theMap.get(map(a, b)).evaluate();
}
```

Normally, I'd arrange for setUp to be invoked from elsewhere, but as the assumption was that this was a one-time test, it might as well be here. If the versionFour method were to be invoked several times, it would certainly be better to move invocation of *setUp* to some initialization code.

Well, using a gigantic hammer to drive a tiny nail, I've kept my promise: really terrible code. No. Wait. Polymorphic code. I'll also note that in order to create this example, I wrote five versions, totaling about 100 lines, with an approximately equal number of lines of test. Yes, I eat my own oatmeal. The tests were essential, both in getting the map function right and in catching a big conceptual error.

Note also, that if the situation calls for it, you can use the Hash Map to obtain a value that is retained in a *currentTest* field so that the state of the computation can be retained.

There are harder cases than this one to transform to polymorphism. One of the hardest is when decisions need to be made based on primitive input values.

The point of this, however, is really just to show the difference between ad hoc and polymorphic code. The ad hoc code has the messy stuff in separate methods, or separate clauses of an IF. The polymorphic code has it in separate objects. The ad hoc decision is via some sort of a test of an expression or the value of a flag. The polymorphic code finds other ways to make the selection and, depending on the situation that may be natural (as in the CalculatorModel) or artificial, as here.

But it is fun to wrestle with problems like this. They can expand your knowledge and skill even beyond the task at hand.

However, the more important skill is to be able to write polymorphic code in the original, rather than doing a later transformation. That takes practice as does any valuable skill.

Your Turn

You might like to give the Polymorphism Challenge a try. Three programs that I think are interesting will be presented, but with no attempt to give them a polymorphic structure. You might try to remove as many IF statements as you can in these and then judge whether the result is an improvement or not. Most of these can be attacked with something like the HashMap example given above, but are a bit easier and more natural. The example above has an infinite space in which the decision had to be made. Here it will be very limited, making it more natural to put the options into a Map.

I think the programs are interesting in their own right, as they introduce important ideas in computing. One introduces a common compiling technique called *recursive descent parsing*. The second uses a dynamically constructed binary tree in which to hold its data. The third program is a simulation of the spread of disease in a population. Two of them, at least, are good vehicles for extension to expand the student's learning and skill.

Recursive Descent

Recursive Descent Parsing is a technique for building either a compiler or an interpreter for a language that is defined by a certain kind of grammar. We will let you explore the details, including why it won't always work. Here we will build an *interpreter* for algebraic expressions. The program will produce a result from a textual description such as 3 + 5 * 2. For this expression it should produce 13, of course. The operators will be addition, subtraction, multiplication, division, and modulo. Modulo gives the integer division remainder. Additionally, the program will respect the normal precedence of the operators, with multiplication having precedence over addition, for example. So, 5 + 3 * 2 should produce 11, not 16. Parentheses are used to override the normal precedence.

This and the other programs here can be downloaded from the URL given earlier. Most include test suites.

The challenge is to remove most of the IF statements. It is possible to remove all but two of them using HashMaps. It is also useful to first create objects to represent the operators.

The program is structured around the following grammar:

```
<expression> ::= <term> <moreTerms>

<term> ::= <factor> <moreFactors>

<moreTerms> ::= "" | ( "+" | "-" ) <term> <moreTerms>

<factor> ::= number | "(" <expression> ")" | "-" <factor>
           | "+" <factor>

<moreFactors> ::= "" | ( "*" | "/" | "%") <factor> <moreFactors>
```

Each statement above is called a *production* and a *grammar* is a list of productions. Each production has a left and a right hand side separated by ::=, which is read "can be" or "has the structure of". A (somewhat restricted definition of a) grammar is a collective definition of the structure of each of the terms on the left sides of its productions, but especially the left side of the first production. So, this is primarily a definition of the structure of <expression>. The vertical stroke is read as "or". Things in quotes, and the special case *number*, are called *tokens*. Note that the definitions are potentially recursive, since, for example, <moreFactors> on the left also has <moreFactors> on the right. The term *number*, above is special. It is a token that represents any unsigned integer. We will use the Java Scanner to retrieve these. Scanners use *regular expressions* to determine how they scan. The order of the symbols is significant.

In general, a *parser*, just verifies that an input has a structure that conforms to the grammar; is valid with respect to the grammar.

A *recursive descent* parser is a program that has a parsing method for each of the items on the left sides, called nonterminals, of its grammar. Moreover the right sides tell us *how* to write those methods. So, for example, The parsing method for <expression>

will first invoke the one for <term> and then the one for <moreTerms> since they are written in that order in the production.

The actual input to the program is a sequence of tokens. The "" token implies that an item may be empty: consist of no symbols at all. Thus, <moreFactors> might be empty or it might consist of a multiplication operator followed by <factor> etc.

Actually, our program will do a bit more than *parse*, or determine the structure of the input. It will also produce an integer value at the end by having each of the parsing methods produce an integer that is incorporated into the next. This is what makes it an *interpreter*. It takes a description of an algorithm (an algebraic expression in this case) and executes the algorithm.

We will explain a few aspects of the program below.

```java
package evaluator.com.jbergin;

import java.util.Scanner;

public class Evaluator {

    private String input = "";
    private Scanner scan;

    private String pad(String input){
        input = input.replaceAll("\\)", " ) ");
        input = input.replaceAll("\\(", " ( ");
        input = input.replaceAll("\\*", " * ");
        input = input.replaceAll("/", " / ");
        input = input.replaceAll("\\+", " + ");
        input = input.replaceAll("-", " - ");
        input = input.replaceAll("%", " % ");
        return input;
    }

    public int evaluate(String input) {
        this.input = input;
        scan = new Scanner(pad(input));
```

```java
        return expression();
    }
    public String toString(){
        return input;
    }

    private int expression(){
        return moreTerms(term());
    }

    private int term(){
        return moreFactors(factor());
    }

    private int moreTerms(int leftPart){
        int result = leftPart;
        if(scan.hasNext("[+-]")){
            String next = scan.next();
            int value = term();
            if(next.equals("+")){
                result = leftPart + value;
            } else if(next.equals("-")) {
                result = leftPart - value;
            }
            result = moreTerms(result);
        }
        return result;
    }

    private int factor(){
        int result = 0;
        if(scan.hasNext("-")){
            scan.next();
            return - factor();
        }
        else if(scan.hasNext("\\+")){
            scan.next();
            return factor();
        } else if(scan.hasNext("\\(")){
```

```
                scan.next();
                result = moreTerms(term());
                scan.next("[)]");
            } else {
                result = scan.nextInt();
            }
            return result;
        }

    private int moreFactors(int leftPart){
        int result = leftPart;
        if(scan.hasNext("[*/%]")){
            String next = scan.next();
            int value = factor();
            if(next.equals("*")){
                result =  leftPart * value;
            } else if(next.equals("/")){
                result =  leftPart / value;
            } else if(next.equals("%")){
                result = leftPart % value;
            }
            result = moreFactors(result);
        }
        return result;
    }

}
```

The *pad* method above is used to insert spaces into the input so that we can be assured that the simple Scanner we use won't pick up anything other than a single token. It is possible to make the Scanner more sophisticated instead, but we want to use a simple one, that expects whitespace between tokens. It will be useful to surround, say + with spaces. Then 5+3 will be transformed to 5 + 3 and the scanner will see three tokens, 5, +, and 3, rather than one. Some of the symbols we use, such as "+" and "(" are considered special to a scanner, and so need to be escaped with \. In fact, "\" itself is special both to the scanner and to the *regular expression* we are matching and so we require double escaping. Whew.

Note that in

```
private int term (){
    return moreFactors(factor());
}
```

we are really just saying invoke <factor> first and then send the
result to <moreFactors>. It is just a compact way of saying:

```
private int term (){
    int temp = factor();
    return moreFactors(temp);
}
```

The important idea is that we invoke *factor* first, just as the
grammar says to do, and then *moreFactors*.

The reader should note that we use IF statements in several ways.
One is to guide the parse by looking at the next token that will be
produced by the scanner. The other is to determine how to handle
the various operators. The latter use of IF is easy to remove, but
you might find it useful to use a special form of HashMap to do so.
Normally, if you try to get something from a Map and the key isn't
present, it will return *null* for a value. As you know, I don't like to
see null in a program, nor test for it. A DefaultHashMap is like a
hash map except that when you create it you give it a value to be
returned for any missing key. Normally this might be a NullObject
value, but you can make it more interesting if you like. Here are the
key parts of the DefaultHashMap.

```
public class DefaultHashMap<K, V> implements Map<K, V>{

    private HashMap<K, V> storage = null;
    private V defaultValue = null;
```

```
    public DefaultHashMap(V defaultValue){
        this.defaultValue = defaultValue;
        storage = new HashMap<K, V>();
    }

    @Override
    public V put(K key, V value){
        return storage.put(key, value);
    }

    @Override
    public void clear() {
        storage.clear();
    }

    @Override
    public V get(Object key){
        V result = storage.get(key);
        if(result != null){
            return result;
        }
        return defaultValue;
    }
    ...
```

When you construct such an object, you provide a default value, which is returned by *get* when the underlying storage map doesn't contain the key. Most of the other methods are like *clear,* above, and just pass the message through to the storage map. I have found the DefaultHashMap to be useful in several projects. Note that the *put* method might return null, and often will in this form. It is easy to modify it to return the default value instead. It is left as an exercise.

Note, that this is built using composition. The class does not extend HashMap, but uses a hash map as a field. It is just another implementation of a Map. It IS-A map, but it HAS-A hash map. I normally prefer to build this way. One reason is that I get better control. And if Oracle should change the implementation of

HashMap in some way, my own API doesn't need to change, and I won't be surprised. It is another way of being explicit in my code.

For the student who wants to explore recursive descent parsing at a deeper level, study *predictive* parsing and LL(1) grammars.

While an interpreter, such as we saw above, actually *executes* an algorithm, a *compiler* translates an algorithm into an equivalent one in a different language, instead. It is quite easy to add additional methods to the above interpreter to make it produce a "program" for the operation of a postfix calculator, such as we saw earlier. For example, it might produce this output:

```
((5) + (-(-3-2)*7 ))/3%(2)
Press 5
Press Push
Press 3
Press ChangeSign
Press Push
Press 2
Press Minus
Press ChangeSign
Press Push
Press 7
Press Times
Press Plus
Press Push
Press 3
Press Divide
Press Push
Press 2
Press Modulo
```

Then, the program becomes (also) a compiler, from infix algebraic expressions into postfix operations. Note that a few of the push operations above (such as the third) are redundant and cause errors, at least on a Hewlett-Packard calculator. It would take a bit more work to omit them. I'll leave that for your exploration. You might also want to research how to incorporate other operators into such a grammar. Especially higher precedence operators.

The Animal Game

This project is an interactive game in which the program will *learn* while playing, which makes its play ever more sophisticated the more it plays. It also illustrates the construction and traversal of binary trees.

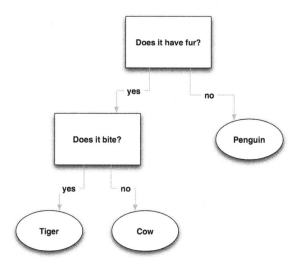

The game proceeds as follows. First the program asks the user to think of an animal. It then asks a series of questions, which the user is expected to answer honestly with *yes* or *no*. Starting at the root of the tree the program moves down one branch or the other (yes or no branches). This continues until the program reaches a leaf of the tree, which represents an animal. It then asks if that animal is the one the user thought of. If so, the program "wins", otherwise the user wins. However if the program loses it then asks the user about the animal so that it can extend the tree for the next play. This program is already rich in objects, as it has distinct classes for the internal, *question*, nodes and the leaf, *animal*, nodes. The program will also save the current state when the user indicates the end of play. In saving, it uses a *postorder* tree walk to create the output file. At startup, it reads the file and uses a stack to recreate the tree. Since this is an interactive game, no test suite is shown here, but one is provided with the download. The test file will demonstrate two different ways to capture standard input and output to enable regression testing.

This program uses IF statements in two different ways. One use is to nicely format the responses given by the program. My polymorphic version doesn't try to remove these. The other use determines the process of the game and the structure of the output when the game is saved. These can all be removed by defining additional classes so that distinct behaviors reside in distinct objects.

Since there are two classes for the nodes, we use an interface to define their structure. This interface arose piecemeal, as I developed the ideas here iteratively.

```
package com.jbergin.animal;

import java.io.BufferedReader;
import java.io.BufferedWriter;

public interface Node {
    public String question();
    public Node play(BufferedReader in);
    public void saveTree(BufferedWriter animals);
}
```

The interior, question, nodes are the simpler variety.

```
package com.jbergin.animal;

import java.io.BufferedReader;
import java.io.BufferedWriter;
import java.io.IOException;

/** This is an internal binary node of the tree. It represents
 *  a question such as "Does it bite?". Play proceeds
 *  down one path in the tree from root to leaf, depending on how
 *  the user answers the questions.
 *  @author jbergin
 *
 */
public class QuestionNode implements Node {
```

```java
    private String question;
    private Node noChild;
    private Node yesChild;
    BufferedReader theReader;

    public QuestionNode(String question, Node yes, Node no){
        // e.g. Does it have fur?
        this.question = question;
        noChild = no;
        yesChild = yes;
    }


    @Override
    public String question() {
        return question;
    }


    @Override
    public void saveTree(BufferedWriter animals){
        yesChild.saveTree(animals);
        noChild.saveTree(animals);
        try {
            animals.write("node: " + question);
            animals.newLine();
        } catch (IOException e) {
            System.out.println(
            "Error writing to animals file: " + question);
        }
    }


    @Override
    public Node play(BufferedReader in) {
        theReader = in;
        System.out.println(question());
        String answer;
        try {
            answer = in.readLine();
            if(answer.toLowerCase().contains("no")){
```

```
                noChild = noChild.play(theReader);
            }
            else {
                yesChild = yesChild.play(theReader);
            }
        } catch (IOException e) {
            System.out.println("Error getting response.");
            e.printStackTrace();
        }
        return this;
    }

}
```

A question node has two children, the *yes child* and the *no child*, each representing an answer to the question posed by the node. Play descends the tree recursively according to the answer given to the question. Play will eventually reach a leaf of the tree. Note that *play* potentially replaces one of the child nodes.

The leaf, or animal, nodes are a bit more complex, since they also need to handle additional communication with the user in case the tree needs to be extended. The animal nodes have no child nodes since they represent the leaves of the tree.

```
package com.jbergin.animal;

import java.io.BufferedReader;
import java.io.BufferedWriter;
import java.io.IOException;
import java.util.HashSet;
import java.util.Set;

/** This is a leaf node of the tree and represents an animal,
 * such as "tiger".
 * @author jbergin
 *
```

```
*/
public class AnimalNode implements Node{

    private String animal;
    String prefix = "a ";
    private static final Set<Character> vowels =
        new HashSet<Character>();

    public AnimalNode(String animal){ // e.g. "octopus"
        this.animal = animal.trim();
        if(vowels.contains(
            Character.toLowerCase(this.animal.charAt(0))
            )){
            prefix = "an ";
        }
    }


    @Override
    public String question(){ // e.g. Is it a penguin?
        return "Is it " + prefix + animal + "?";
    }


    @Override
    public void saveTree(BufferedWriter animals){
        try {
            animals.write("leaf: " + animal);
            animals.newLine();
        } catch (IOException e) {
            System.out.println("Error writing to
                animals file: " + animal);
        }
    }


    private boolean yesQuery(String query, BufferedReader in)
            throws IOException{
        System.out.println(query);
        return ! in.readLine().toLowerCase().contains("no");
    }
```

```java
private String query(String query, BufferedReader in)
        throws IOException{
    System.out.println(query);
    return in.readLine();
}


/** Make sure the question suggested by the user
 * actually reads like a question. Capitalize the
 * first word and append a question mark if needed.
 */
private String doctor(String question){
    String result = question.trim();
    Character first = result.charAt(0);
    first = Character.toUpperCase(first);
    result= first + result.substring(1);
    Character last = result.charAt(result.length()-1);
    if(! last.equals('?')){
        result += '?';
    }
    return result;
}


/** Get information about the user's animal create add a new
 * node for the tree for that animal.
 * @param in the source of the user input
 * @return the question node that is created. It will be
 * attached to the parent after play returns.
 * @throws IOException
 */
private Node getNode(BufferedReader in) throws IOException{
    String animal = query("What animal were you thinking of?",
        in).trim();
    String newPrefix = "a ";
    if(vowels.contains(Character.toLowerCase(
        animal.charAt(0)))){
        newPrefix = "an ";
    }

    String question = query(
        "What is a yes-no question that will distinguish " +
            newPrefix + animal +
        " from " + prefix + this.animal + "?", in);
```

```java
        question = doctor(question);
        AnimalNode newLeaf = new AnimalNode(animal);
        boolean isYes = yesQuery("What would be the answer for "+
            newPrefix + animal + "?", in);
        Node result = this;
        if(isYes){
            result = new QuestionNode(
                question, newLeaf, this);
        } else {
            result = new QuestionNode(
                question, this, newLeaf);
        }
        return result;
    }

    static{
        vowels.add('a');
        vowels.add('e');
        vowels.add('i');
        vowels.add('o');
        vowels.add('u');
    }

    /* If the user's animal is the same as the animal in this node,
     * the computer "wins". Otherwise it "loses" and asks the user
     * about the animal to extend the tree for the next game.
     *
     * @see com.jbergin.animal.Node#play(java.io.BufferedReader)
     */
    @Override
    public Node play(BufferedReader in) {
        boolean yes = false;
        Node result = this;
        try {
            yes  = yesQuery(question(), in);
            if(yes){
                System.out.println("I win.");
            }
            else {
                System.out.println("You win.");
```

```
                    result = getNode(in );
            }
        } catch (IOException e) {
            System.out.println("Error getting response.");
            e.printStackTrace();
        }
        return result;
    }
}
```

This code may also be downloaded so that you can play with it.

Note that the *play* method of AnimalNode either returns the *this* object, or creates a new QuestionNode of which *this* is a child.

Finally, we need a class to hold our main method and to direct the action initially.

```
package com.jbergin.animal;

import java.io.BufferedWriter;
import java.io.File;
import java.io.FileReader;
import java.io.FileWriter;
import java.io.IOException;
import java.io.BufferedReader;
import java.io.InputStreamReader;
import java.util.Stack;

public class AnimalGame {

    private QuestionNode root;
    private BufferedReader in = new BufferedReader(
        new InputStreamReader(System.in));
    private File animalFile = new File("animalDB.txt");

    private boolean playAgain() throws IOException{
        System.out.println("\nPlay again?");
```

```java
            String answer = in.readLine();
            return ! answer.trim().toLowerCase().contains("no");
    }


    public AnimalGame(
        String question, String yesAnswer, String noAnswer) {
        if(! animalFile.exists()){
            root = new QuestionNode(
                question,
                new AnimalNode(yesAnswer),
                new AnimalNode(noAnswer));
            return;
        }
        Stack<Node> builder = new Stack<Node>();
        BufferedReader animals = null;
        try {
            animals = new BufferedReader(
                new FileReader(animalFile));
            String line;
            while((line = animals.readLine()) != null){
                if(line.startsWith("leaf: ")){
                    AnimalNode aNode =
                    new AnimalNode(line.replaceFirst("leaf: ", ""));
                    builder.push(aNode);
                } else{
                    Node falseNode = builder.pop();
                    Node trueNode = builder.pop();
                    QuestionNode aNode =
                    new QuestionNode(
                        line.replaceFirst("node: ", ""),
                        trueNode, falseNode);
                    builder.push(aNode);
                }
            }
            animals.close();
        } catch (IOException e) {
            System.out.println(
                "Sorry, can't play. File problem.");
            e.printStackTrace();
            System.exit(1);
        }
```

```
        root = (QuestionNode) builder.pop();
    }

    public void saveTree(BufferedWriter animals){
        root.saveTree(animals);
    }

    public void play() throws IOException{
        do{
            System.out.println(
            "Think of an Animal. Answer questions with yes or no.");
            root.play(in);
        }while(playAgain());
    }

    public static void main(String[] args) throws IOException {
        AnimalGame game = new AnimalGame("Does it have fur?",
            "fox", "penguin");
        game.play();
        System.out.println();
        BufferedWriter animals = new BufferedWriter(
            new FileWriter(game.animalFile));
        game.saveTree(animals);
        animals.close();
    }
}
```

While trying to make this code simple, I let an important flaw get through. It assumes, in several places, that a user response that doesn't contain "no" is treated as a "yes." This, in fact, is how serious attacks are made on software. The software makes some assumption that isn't warranted. It would be better to test that the user's response is precisely correct: "yes", or "no." As it is written, a user response of "Nothing could be more true", likely indicating a "yes" answer, would be treated as a "no" instead.

It might be more interesting if a fixed set of responses were allowed, say, "yes", "si", "ja", "oui." A HashSet could be used to check for these and the program could loop until an acceptable answer is given. A HashMap could, instead, map responses to actions, and a DefaultHashMap could handle incorrect responses.

Also, the fact that I didn't remove those IF statements that are used only to determine what is presented to the user, does not mean that these are less important. In fact, in many programs, the user interface is the *most* important thing and great care should be taken in developing it. That is why I included these IF statements in the program. It is better to say "an octopus" than "a octopus" in English. So don't neglect little (or big) tweaks that make the user experience more comfortable. And, if you are new to building software for others to use, you need to be aware that often the hardest job of all is correctly responding to incorrect input. We have already seen that a test suite might be longer than the code that it tests. But, it is also common for error detection, response, and correction is the biggest part of the code itself. This is usually true in compilers, for example, though optimization code can also be quite extensive. When you build for yourself you can usually respond correctly to your own errors, but a user who is not a programmer will just be mystified when your program does something that seems odd to them.

Simulation

Lastly we will see a simulation program that is intended to give some insight into how disease spreads in a population. It illustrates computing in the service of science and public policy. The population can have various characteristics that affect the spread, as can the disease. The code presented here is a bit more than just a program. It is really a framework intended to be modified with additional (essential) complexity added. For example, the model of a disease allows it to transform over time, but none of the code here actually exploits that possibility. Nor do we account for recovery from a disease. The user/programmer is invited to explore and gain insight. The code can also be wrapped into something larger, perhaps a study that runs the simulation repeatedly, gathering statistical information that a single run cannot provide. We will illustrate random numbers, arrays, generics, and a few other coding techniques.

We start with two interfaces that set the structure of the exploration. The first, and simplest, defines a Disease:

```
package com.jbergin.disease;

/** A disease that may be introduced into a population
 * @param <T> A change measure, such as time
 */
public interface Disease<T> {

    /** Set the probability that contact with an infected
     * "location" will result in infection.
     * @param probability the probability of infection, in
     * range [0.0, 1.0]
     */
    public void setInfectionProbability(double probability);

    /** The current probability of infection
     * @return the probability that contact with a location will
     * result in infection.
     */
    public double infectionProbability();

    /** Some diseases transform over time. This permits signaling
     * the disease that it should update itself.
     * @param value value needed to drive the change
     */
    public void update(T value);
}
```

This interface is generic and requires that a parameter be supplied when a (non-generic) class implements it. The parameter gives the type of information passed to the *update* method. A simple disease (as we will see) might just use Integer, so that *update* can be passed an int, but it can be an object of an arbitrary class.

Disease is very simple. It contains a probability that contact will result in infection. An implementation of the interface will likely have constructors that may set this probability, but we also permit it to be modified. Often the probability will just be a field of the object, but need not be. Here is a realization of this interface:

65

```
package com.jbergin.disease;

public class SimpleDisease implements Disease<Integer> {

    private double probability = 0.0d;

    public SimpleDisease(double initialProbability){
        this.probability = initialProbability;
        normalize();
    }

    public SimpleDisease(){
        //nothing
    }

    private final void normalize(){
        probability =  Math.min(1.0, probability);
        this.probability = Math.max(0, probability);
    }

    @Override
    public void setInfectionProbability(double probability) {
        this.probability = probability;
        normalize();
    }

    @Override
    public double infectionProbability() {
        return probability;
    }

    @Override
    public void update(Integer value) {
        //nothing
    }
}
```

An object of this type has a fixed probability, though we do permit it to be changed. *Update,* however does nothing. We only guarantee that the probability is between 0 and 1. Note that a SimpleDisease created with the default constructor can't actually infect the population, since its probability of infection is zero. A more interesting disease is one that becomes less virulent when updated:

```java
package com.jbergin.disease;

public class FadingDisease implements Disease<Integer> {
    private double probability = 0.0d;

    public FadingDisease(double initialProbability){
        this.probability = initialProbability;
        normalize();
    }

    private final void normalize(){
        probability =  Math.min(1.0, probability);
        probability = Math.max(0, probability);
    }

    @Override
    public void setInfectionProbability(double probability) {
        this.probability = probability;
        normalize();
    }

    @Override
    public double infectionProbability() {
        return probability;
    }

    @Override
    public void update(Integer value) {
        value = Math.max(1, value);
        probability /= Math.max(1, value);
        normalize();
    }
}
```

Perhaps you think this model of a disease is overly simplified. If so, you are welcome to add additional methods to the interface; perhaps something about the probability of recovery from the disease. It is really just a framework for exploration.

Note that *normalize* is final. Thus it is safe to call from a constructor.

Populations are much more interesting, though we shall see a discussion about that below.

```java
package com.jbergin.disease;
import java.util.Set;

/** A population into which a disease may be introduced to study
 * how it spreads. A population has a "shape" which helps
 * determine how a disease spreads. A population may be mobile or
 * not. If it is mobile, a disease may jump over distance,
 * otherwise it spreads only locally. In this model the state of a
 * population location is either immune, infected, or
 * available for infection (healthy).
 * @param <P> a "point" or "location" within the population
 * @param <D> a "direction", usually from a location
 * @param <T> a "change" measure, such as time
 */
public interface Population<P, D, T> {

    /** The number of cells in the population
     * @return the number of cells
     */
    public int size();

    /** Try to infect this location with the probability associated
     * with the disease
     * @param location the location to be (possibly) infected
     */
    public void infect(P location);

    /** Introduce a disease into a random location of a population
     * @param <T> a change measure such as time
     * @param disease the disease to be introduced
     */
```

```java
public void introduce(Disease<T> disease);


/** The current number of infected cells
 * @return the number of infected cells
 */
public int numberInfected();
/** How many cells are neither infected nor immune
 * @return the number of cells available to be infected
 */
public int numberHealthy();


/** How many cells have been immunized
 * @return the number of immunized cells
 */
public int numberImmune();


/** Spread the disease for a certain number of cycles.
 * On a cycle an infected cell will attempt
 * to infect its neighbors
 * @param cycles the number of cycles to run the simulation
 */
public void spread(int cycles);


/** Immunize a proportion of the population against the disease
 * (assumes only one disease)
 * @param percentage the probability a given cell is immunized.
 * @return the number actually immunized
 */
public int immunize(double percentage);


/** Permits members of a cell to visit, and possibly infect,
 * other random cells in the population
 * @param howMany the number of cells that "travel" and thus
 * spread disease to the destination, or get infected there.
 */
public void shuffle(int howMany);


/** Create an immunization barrier in the population in a given
 * direction starting at a given location. If
 * the population wraps back on itself the barrier will also,
```

```
 * back to the location. Otherwise it will extend to the
 * "edge" of the population. This can be used to create
 * "islands" in the population.
 * @param direction The direction to which the barrier extends
 * @param location the end of the barrier
 * @param distance the length of the barrier. If 0 it extends
 * to the edge of the population (or wraps around)
 */
public void immunizeFrom(P location, D direction, int
    distance);


/** Once each cycle, spread invokes shuffle. The mobility value
 * determines how many members of the population visit
 * other cells. Set this to 0 to avoid "travel".
 * @param mobility the number of population cells that visit
 * other cells per cycle in the spread method.
 */
public void setMobility(int mobility);


/** The currently infected cells
 * @return a set of infected cells
 */
public Set<P> infected();


/** Determine if a location is infected
 * @param location the location to check
 * @return true if the location is infected
 */
public boolean isInfected(P location);


/** Determine if a location is immune to infection
 * @param location the location to check
 * @return true if the location is immune
 */
public boolean isImmune(P location);


/** Determine if the location is available for infection
 * @param location the location to check
 * @return true if the location is available for infection
 */
```

```
    public boolean isHealthy(P location);
}
```

A population can be visualized as a collection of "cells" and each cell has a given State, one of healthy, infected, or immune. A basic assumption here is that there is only one disease, since it doesn't distinguish "infected by which disease." Each cell has neighbors determined by the shape of the population. For example, if the population is like a two dimensional array a cell will have eight neighbors, unless it is along an edge. In a spherical population with an "array like" grid, it will always have eight. None of the examples of populations that I've built have any real notion of distance, however. Other implementations could provide that, of course. The *state* of the cells is defined by an enumeration. The symbol associated with a state is only used in printing out a population so that you can get a visual feel of the situation.

```
package com.jbergin.disease;

public enum State{
    IMMUNE(" - "),
    INFECTED(" + "),
    HEALTHY(" . ");

    private String symbol;

    State(String symbol){
        this.symbol = symbol;
    }

    public String toString(){
        return symbol;
    }
}
```

Another possible state might be *RECOVERED*.

The basic characteristics of a population are determined by three parameters, P, D, and T. The last is used to determine the characteristics of the diseases permitted in the population. The P parameter determines the characteristics of the cells themselves. In the supplied example we will see only *Point* (from java.awt). However, any class can be used here and an elaborate one could provide for disease recovery over time, or other things. In the examples, once a cell is infected it will remain infected, and can infect others, for the duration of the simulation. The D parameter determines direction in the population and is used by the *immunizeFrom* method to build barriers to infection. For example, an immunization barrier that extends completely across a population will prevent neighbor-to-neighbor spread of a disease. You can use this method to simulate the effect of oceans in real populations. Most diseases don't spread over oceans in the absence of travel. In many populations, the directions permitted (as determined by the class substituted for the D parameter) are just North, East, South, and West. In a linear population, however, such as a one dimensional array, the directions might be only East and West. Examples are provided in the code you can download. Our usual Direction class, however, is just a simple enum.

```
package com.jbergin.disease;

public enum Direction {
    NORTH,
    EAST,
    SOUTH,
    WEST;
}
```

A more elaborate version might include NorthEast, etc. It could even include 360 degrees of compass directions.

The examples provided with this book show several different populations, all based in some way on an array of one or two dimensions. Here we will see only a simple planar world with edges, modeling a bounded two dimensional world. A disease cannot spread past the edge. It is possible, however, to modify this in many ways. For example, if you *connect* the left and right edges together so that a disease might spread off the left side and on to the right, you get a tubular world. If you also connect the top and bottom you get a torus. A spherical world is a bit more complex, but the details are shown in the downloaded code. A somewhat weirder world would be to connect the left and right, but reverse the orientation, giving a Möbius band. Then, spreading off the left side near the top would come back on the right side near the bottom. A planar world with width ten, however, looks something like the following, just as you expect:

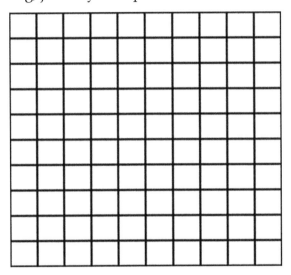

The PlanarPopulation class is quite long. We will show the important parts below. First we have the implementing fields. Note that it uses the Point class for the locations, and the Direction class shown above for the D parameter. The *population* array will be square, with *width* cells on each side. Since we want to process this array many times using FOR loops, we define a *range* array that provides a convenient iterator for the population itself. The *shuffleNumber* determines how many cells may "travel" to remote locations as the simulation progresses (see method *spread*). The constructor initializes everything and shows how we will use the *range* variable.

```
public class PlanarPopulation implements Population<Point,
Direction, Integer> {

    private int width = 0;
    private State [][] population = null;
    private Random random = new Random();
    private Disease<Integer> disease = null;
    private Set<Point> infected = new HashSet<Point>();
    private int[] range = null;
    private int shuffleNumber = 0;

    /** Create a planar world
     * @param width the width (and height) of the world.
     */
    public PlanarPopulation(int width){
        this.width = width;
        this.population = new State[width][width];
        this.range = new int[width];
        for(int i = 0; i < width; ++i){
            this.range[i] = i;
        }
        for(int i : this.range) {
            for(int j : this.range){
                this.population[i][j] = State.HEALTHY;
            }
        }
    }
}
```

Once we create a population, we might use it as follows:

```
package com.jbergin.disease;

import java.awt.Point;

public class PlanarPopulationTrial {
```

```
public static void  main(String[] args){
    PlanarPopulation population = new PlanarPopulation(15);
    population.setMobility(3);
    Point where = new Point(10, 5);
    population.immunizeFrom(where, Direction.NORTH, 0);
    Disease<Integer> disease = new SimpleDisease(0.6);
    int immunized = population.immunize(0.3);
    population.introduce(disease);
    population.spread(6);
    System.out.println("Number infected: "
        + population.numberInfected());
    System.out.println(population.toString());
    System.out.println("Number available but not infected: "
        + population.numberHealthy());
    System.out.println("Number immunized: "
        + population.numberImmune());
}
}
```

Here the population has 225 cells (its *size*), and the mobility is set to 3. This will initialize the shuffleNumber field. We then erect a partial barrier to infection by immunizing in the North direction from cell (10, 5). Note that our counting of cells starts at 0, so the rows and columns are numbered 0 through 14.

Next we create a simple disease with a 0.6 probability of infecting a given healthy cell and then randomly immunize 30% of the population. Then the disease is introduced into the population at a random location. If it happens to be an immune location, no changes will occur when we run the simulation.

Finally we run the simulation through six cycles. In each cycle some locations may visit other random locations, possibly affecting them and all infected cells try to infect their neighbors, limited by the virulence (probability of spread) of the disease. Then we just look at the population and some of its statistics.

One of the key things we want to do with a population is introduce a disease into a random location.

```
    @Override
    public void introduce(Disease<Integer> disease) {
        this.disease =  disease;
        Point p = randomLocation();
        System.out.println("Introducing disease at: " + p);
        infect(p);
    }
```

This method saves the disease, obtains a random location, using a private method, and then passes that point to the *infect* method. The *infect* method is used uniformly to infect cells, rather than simply setting the cell's state to infected.

```
    @Override
    public void infect(Point location){
        if(includes(location)
                && isHealthy(location)
                && this.random.nextDouble()
                    < this.disease.infectionProbability()){
            this.population[location.x][location.y] =
                State.INFECTED;
            this.infected.add((Point)location.clone());
            System.out.println("infecting: " + location);
        }
    }
```

The print statements here are not essential, of course, but let the user follow the course of the simulation. The reason for always delegating the infect process to a single method should now be clear. There is a fair amount of work that should always accompany the operation, such as saving the location in the *infected* set. Note how we use the *random* object to control the infection. *NextDouble* returns a value in the range [0.0, 1.0] so it works well as a probability without scaling. The *includes* method is also private and just guarantees that a location is within the population array. The need to clone the point is discussed below.

Once a disease is introduced there will be (zero or) one infected cell. We can then spread the disease through a number of cycles.

```
@Override
public void spread(int cycles) {
    for(int i = 0; i < cycles; i++){
        HashSet<Point> temp = (HashSet<Point>)
            ((HashSet<Point>) this.infected).clone();
        for(Point p : temp){
            shuffle(this.shuffleNumber);
            spreadFrom(p);
        }
    }
}
```

For each cycle this method clones the infected set. Yes, all the casting is necessary, since *clone* is only known to return an Object, but we need to assure the system that it is really cloning a HashSet and so the object is, indeed, a HashSet. We need the clone, since we will indirectly infect some cells, which will modify the infected set. You cannot iterate over a collection and simultaneously modify it.

We invoke two methods here, *shuffle* and *spreadFrom*. Shuffle, lets some of the cells "visit" other cells, possibly passing the infection. The locations are chosen randomly.

```
@Override
public void shuffle(int howMany) {
    for(int i = 0; i < howMany; ++i){
        Point from = randomLocation();
        Point to = randomLocation();
        if(isImmune(from) || isImmune(to)){
            return;
        }
        if(isInfected(from)){
            infect(to);
        }
        if(isInfected(to)){
            infect(from);
        }
    }
```

```
        }
```

The private *spreadFrom* method will, from an infected cell, try to infect the neighbors in the array, of which there are up to eight, depending on the location; fewer if it is at an edge.

```java
private void spreadFrom(Point location){
    Point temp = new Point(0, 0);
    for(int i = location.x - 1; i < location.x + 2; ++i){
        for(int j = location.y - 1; j < location.y + 2; ++j){
            temp.move(i, j);
            infect(temp);
        }
    }
}
```

Now we can see the need to clone the point in *infect*. The *move* operation of a point just modifies the point. It doesn't give us a new point object. At other places we just set the x and y fields of the point directly, since Points are not encapsulated. But since the object remains the same and we are storing them in a set, we want a value there for each location, not for each point object used to refer to a location. Cloning gives us a new object, but we apply it only when we need to. This points out a danger of using mutable objects.

We immunize a fraction of the population with immunize.

```java
@Override
public int immunize(double percentage){
    percentage = normalize(percentage);
    int result = 0;
    for(int i: this.range){
        for(int j: this.range){
            if(this.population[i][j] == State.HEALTHY
                    && this.random.nextDouble() < percentage){
                this.population[i][j] = State.IMMUNE;
```

```
            result++;
          }
        }
      }
      return result;
  }
```

Normalizing a percentage just guarantees it is the range [0.0, 1.0]. Comparing a random double with the percentage gives us the approximately correct proportion of immune cells.

The final method we will discuss here is the *immunizeFrom* method. It is the most complex of our methods. It is a SWITCH with a case for each possible direction, with guards that we don't try to go beyond the edge of the population. Remember also, that a distance of 0 implies that the barrier should extend to the edge in the given direction. We use the ?: operator here.

```
      @Override
      public void immunizeFrom(Point location,
              Direction direction, int distance){
        distance = Math.abs(distance);
        int endpoint;
        switch(direction){
        case NORTH: {
          endpoint = distance == 0?
              0 :
              Math.max(0, location.y - distance + 1);
          for(int i = endpoint; i <= location.y; ++i){
              if(this.population[location.x][i]
                  == State.HEALTHY) {
                  this.population[location.x][i]
                      = State.IMMUNE;
              }
          }
        }
        break;
        case EAST: {
```

```
                endpoint = distance == 0?
                    this.width :
                    Math.min(this.width, location.x + distance );
                for(int i = location.x; i < endpoint; ++i){
                    if(this.population[i][location.y]
                        == State.HEALTHY) {

                        this.population[i][location.y]
                            = State.IMMUNE;
                    }
                }
            }
            break;
            case SOUTH: {
                endpoint = distance == 0?
                    this.width:
                    Math.min(this.width, location.y + distance );
                for(int i = location.y; i < endpoint; ++i){
                    if(this.population[location.x][i]
                        == State.HEALTHY) {

                        this.population[location.x][i]
                            = State.IMMUNE;
                    }
                }
            }
            break;
            case WEST: {
                endpoint = distance == 0?
                    0 :
                    Math.max(0, location.x - distance + 1);
                for(int i = endpoint; i <= location.x; ++i){
                    if(this.population[i][location.y]
                        == State.HEALTHY) {

                        this.population[i][location.y]
                            = State.IMMUNE;
                    }
                }
            }
            break;
        }
    }
```

Not that it is necessary, but the FOR loop in each case provides increasing indices. Thus in each case we compute one endpoint in the direction in which the barrier should proceed. If the distance given is zero, it is one of the edge points. Otherwise it is *distance* cells away, but not beyond the edge. We then just set all healthy sells to immune.

The other examples of populations, such as a spherical population are broadly similar to this one. Each of them can give insight about how disease spreads under different conditions. Of course you need more that 225 cells in your population to be at all realistic, and you need to make several runs, averaging results to learn anything meaningful. This is an essential feature of randomized simulations.

If you want to try to make this program more polymorphic, you should first spend some time thinking about its structure. Does it have good overall structure? I think it can be improved greatly with a little thought. Note that all of the important methods are in the population class. Is that best? How much of the functionality can you move out to the State and Direction classes? Making the Direction class richer might let you avoid the SWITCH statement just above, for example. The Disease classes don't do very much either. They provide no services. The fact that I named one method *setInfectionProbability* emphasizes this. Can you pass some of the population functionality over to Disease? Should we require more of our locations, here just Points? Perhaps the array should not contain States, but some richer concept that contains a State. That would complicate the parameterization of the Population interface, however. But once you start to move the functionality, polymorphism becomes easier and more valuable. There are a lot of possibilities. You could have a lot of fun with it.

But you can have fun with this concept in other ways as well. Instead of a two dimensional array you could use three, or more, dimensions. In three you have a cubical population. You might try to build it into a model of how heat disperses through a solid. In three dimensions if you connect a pair of opposite faces you have something like a solid torus. You could explore sparse arrays. You could have sets, rather than arrays of cells, connected in some kind of graph. With a graph you might interpret it as a communication network and explore rumor and meme spread. More fun.

This project would benefit from a GUI, of course. If you want to explore that, I'd suggest that you let the Population classes extend Observable. Then, when a change occurs, you can signal the GUI (its Observer) so that the view updates seemingly by magic. A GUI could be added to any of the calculators in a similar way. Below is a representation of a run of the above program as output by a GUI. This is the final result, with the darker cells being infected. It is interesting to watch it run, also, as the infection spreads in the population.

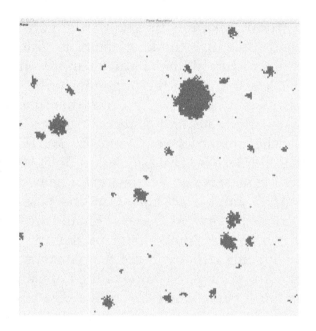

Programming

Programming Programming

Programming Programming Programming

Programming Programming

Programming

Building Software: Work and Fun

I build software because I enjoy it. It is, or was, part of my job. So, for me, it has always been both work and fun. But you often need to distinguish the two. If you build software at someone else's direction, you give up a great deal of control over the vision. That is fine. You still want to be creative, just to keep your mind active. But you express your creativity in the *how* of it, not the *what*. The client, or the manager, of the development process determines *what* is to be built and tries to also determine how much will be spent and when the process is finished. As a developer you will have little control over that. If the product to be built is determined by a complete specification, you just attempt to build to that specification. If it is specified by stories, you try to build to the customer's understanding of each story. This can be fun or not, depending on the overall situation. Often it is just work.

When you program an assignment for a professor, he or she is your customer and is in control of what you should build. Normally you should do just that and not try to embellish it with flights of fancy, gargoyles and such. Of course, gargoyles may be part of the assignment in some cases, but don't lose track of the distinction.

When you build for yourself, however, you are in complete control. You determine both the *what* and the *how*. This is almost always fun. You can follow your dream. You can switch directions, circle back. You can determine when you are done. If you are happy with a personal project, thinking you are done and want to turn it into a product for others to use, be aware you are only half done. Your user interface will probably need lots of work.

But occasionally it is possible to combine work and fun. One of the appeals, for me, of agile development, is that the entire product is not specified completely before I come into the process, usually as a coach. The customer doesn't need to have a completely detailed design at the beginning of the project. A vague idea is actually enough, if he or she or they are willing to be flexible.

For me, the sweet spot of developing for others in the agile environment is a situation in which the product to be delivered cannot, even it principle, be specified completely before development begins. This is true more often than many are willing to admit. In the real world of business, and science, and medicine, and, well, whatever, thing change. Often they change rapidly. If someone specifies a product completely and then it takes six months or a year to build it, then it may not be needed anymore. At least not needed in that form. I travelled in China a few years ago. China was in a situation of extremely rapid development. I saw several situations in which new buildings, never used, were being torn down to free space to build something different. The needs changed, and the buildings didn't fit the current needs. Too often, traditionally designed software is like that.

Normally, when I build software for myself, I start with only a vague idea of where I want to get to. The Karel J Robot simulators were like that. I had a simple picture in my head that I thought would work. So I started to build. But at every step I evaluated what I had. Often enough I didn't like what I had built and changed it. My goal kept shifting. At the end of the process I was very happy with it, but it was only loosely related to the original vision. That was fun, though it took longer than if I'd kept to the original idea. I could have had something worse much quicker. Not a big advantage.

I like customers who are willing to assess the results of a development as it goes along. They can assess it for quality, of course, but it is equally important that they assess it for suitability. Most people who sponsor software are not the actual users of the software. Often they know a lot about the users, more than I do, I hope. But they probably don't know everything. So, periodically, the software in development should be put to real users for evaluation and the product and process re-guided depending on what is learned.

It is also essential to periodically stop and take some time to look at how your *process* is working. You want to learn what is working and what isn't so that you can improve and not just keep going in the wrong direction. Hence Retrospectives.

One of the big projects that I consulted on, for a large (very large) company, MBI Inc. (Massively Big Industry), started out as "We need X and we are sure that Y will not be a factor." The project was projected to last about eight months. In week three, or thereabouts, focus changed and it turned out it was *all* about Y. The early development proved that to the sponsor, who would not have become aware had the process developed normally, with specification, design, programming, testing, etc. They needed to see and operate the partly-built program itself to see that their conception was incorrect and would not fill their need. The project turned out to be so successful that it generated an important change in the company itself. MBI Inc. has become more agile, and not just in software development.

Most people think of Agile Development as a set of specific practices to build software; pair programming, test first, etc. But actually it is a set of principles, from which the practices are derived. One of the principles is "Don't get stuck." Another is "Deliver value continuously." A third is "Continuous feedback." "Embrace change." "Individuals are more important than tools and processes." "Reflection/Retrospectives." "Open communication." There are others. All of these can be applied to any process, not just software. But the actual practices will depend on the context. They won't be the same as those of Agile Software Development.

In the Doctoral program in computing at Pace University, students are encouraged to think of their dissertation as an agile process. Continuous progress. Small steps. High-value steps first. Continuous feedback. Fixed length iterations. Sustainable pace. And more. Students have even been asked to write stories for the next iteration, describing their next steps.

You are encouraged to look at the kinds of things you do yourself and to imagine how you might be more agile in carrying out your tasks. See the Agile Manifesto, referenced in *Polymorphism*.

Think, Grow, Play, ...

More Stories

Here are the additional stories for the Coffee Machine. You can treat each one individually. If you can add each of these, except Story 10 without changing the design, all the better. You will likely want a new class for Story 10, but other things should not need change.

However, before you modify the program, there are a few questions about your current program that are worth answering.

Which component knows the recipe for each product? Which component knows the prices? Is any component a bottleneck in the design, meaning that it needs to communicate with too many other components? Is your functionality in the correct components, or should you move it around a bit for a cleaner program? Depending on your answers you may want to refactor before you continue.

> 7. Soup: It also dispenses soup for $.25

I note that float and double are terrible choices for representing money. Int is a bit better, but *Money*, a class you build, is best. You can avoid absurdities such as negative money, for example.

> 8. Money Accepted: It only takes nickels, dimes, and quarters. To add $0.35, insert a dime and a quarter, for example, or seven nickels.

Of course, if this isn't based on U.S. currency, we would want to accept the Looney or the Quid, perhaps.

> 9 Change Dispensers: Change is returned from special change dispensers, One for each kind of coin. It is not returned from the money inserted.

10. Vendor Interface: It should be possible to increase prices for the products via a vendor interface (not the front panel).

11. Change Needed: It won't dispense product if it can't make change.

Note the interaction with Story 9.

12. Extra Strong: Extra Strong coffee is offered. It has two helpings of coffee.

13. Bills: It takes bills/notes as well as coins. Change is just coins though. The acceptable bills are $1, $5, and $10, only.

14. Refill: It should be possible to fill the ingredient bins (via the vendor interface)

a) Add a fixed amount to every bin.
b) Fill to a predefined optimal level for each bin.
c) Fill (or just add to) an individual bin.

15. Credit Cards: It takes credit/debit cards for the exact amount of a transaction only.

> 16. Report: It provides a report of money earned. It is the sum of sales since last reset.

A more interesting report would include a breakdown of sales by product.

> 17. Future Directions: It gives cappuccino, latte, iced coffee, and a wide range of other coffee drinks and other beverages with weekly specials and a changing menu.

A really good design might accommodate almost all of this without a redesign. Adding additional objects is the preferred method, not needing additional classes or new connections (references) between classes. The vendor story, again, probably does require a new class, of course, and Money if you build it. What similarities are there between the components that you might exploit in simplifying a design?

A really bad design is a Big Ball o' Mud, possibly a single class, that tries to mush it all together. Another looks like an octopus with a central all-knowing, all-seeing controller and some relatively dumb appendages connected to it: warts on a toad. These are bad designs for most programs. A pipeline architecture works occasionally. Each object feeds information to the next in sequence. Connect the ends and you have a cyclic system. The "core" of the system can be on the *control*, or on the *data* controlled. And since data has behavior in object-oriented systems the latter can be a powerful idea.

Sorry, ain't haiku
maybe close, refactor it
come and play again

Big Ideas

A listing of Dr. J's Big Ideas, though they are not original with him: Some were introduced in *Polymorphism*, and some here.

Abstraction: Write code so that you can think in terms of the abstractions in the *problem space*, not the implementation. Think in *problem space*, not *solution space*.

Agility: Apply the agile principles to your normal work practices.

Composition: Prefer to build by composition of objects rather than inheritance.

Creativity Under Constraint: Use artificial constraints to train your mind to overcome any constraint.

Delegation: An object can delegate part of its behavior to another object.

Design Patterns: A vocabulary of design ideas, useful in communication as well as in developing program structure.

Fun: Life is short, it should be fun. But do good work, too.

Immutable: A program with a high proportion of immutable objects is easier to reason about.

Intention Revealing Names: Always. Just do it!

Interfaces: If the language permits, prefer to define the structure of things with interfaces. See Pure Implementation.

Objects: Prefer objects rather than primitives, as it gives you more control.

New Paradigms: Throw away your dusty deck exercises if you want to teach object-oriented programming, or any new paradigm, effectively.

Patterns: Employ known best-practice solutions in your work.

Pair Programming: A big win for productivity and learning.

Peer Evaluation: Members of a team should have the opportunity to evaluate one another. It is best if positive focused.

Polymorphism: An object can change its behavior and yet maintain encapsulation. Strategy and State design patterns enable this.

Problem Space: Name elements of your program using terms from the problem space, not the solution space. Think in terms of the problem, not the solution. Model the problem space.

Pure Implementation: If you implement an interface, don't add additional public methods to the class. If you need additional public methods, extend the interface, instead, and implement that.

Regression Testing: Tests should be automated and executed, at least daily, as a suite. Immediately fix indicated problems.

Retrospectives: Capture and preserve the knowledge of what works and what doesn't in any team activity.

Separate Testing from Code: The tests should not require special scaffolding in the code.

Services: Objects should provide services to clients, rather than values.

Simplicity: Don't introduce inessential complexity.

Stories: Build large applications one feature at a time. Contrast with BDUF (Big Design Up Front) which is also often used.

Test First: Build what you need, but only what you need. Make the test pass.

Unit Testing: Early tests fail when you go wrong later.

User Interface: Pay special attention to the quality of the user experience in your programs.

From Albert Einstein: Imagination is more important than knowledge.

I would add: Hard work is more important than intelligence.

More For Instructors

Here are a few more lessons I think are especially important when teaching students to program in object-oriented languages.

One of the most important is to use classes to build *objects*, not hierarchies. By that I mean, don't use inheritance from concrete classes as a major technique. It is rare. Instead, write interfaces, providing that the language permits it. In Python and Ruby interfaces are not part of the language, but you can still write them informally as a guide to your work. Use an abstract class when a number of classes implementing an interface have common code. Class hierarchies are normally very flat.

Even more important, I believe, is to use composition rather than inheritance for most things. So, the DefaultHashMap was built with an ordinary HashMap as a field, not as a subclass of HashMap. We treat the DefaultHashMap as a new kind of thing, not as a specialization of a HashMap, though in reality that view is reasonable here. But Cylinder as a specialization of Circle is not at all reasonable. Nor is circle as a subclass of point.

Writing interfaces, rather than classes, also helps you to think in terms of naming things in the language of the problem, not the solution. You are less involved in the details of the code when writing an interface. Think in terms of what you want to accomplish, not how to accomplish it. You are less likely to get into the getter-setter mindset when developing an interface.

Prefer to use custom built objects rather than primitives nearly always, even if they are very simple. I've said this many times here, of course. You can create student exercises in which you provide the overall structure and students write simple classes for objects to interact with it. One example that comes to mind is a "Dungeon Game" with Characters, Places, and Things. Students can write new types of Things to be carried by Characters, for example. You can provide the Thing interface, with methods such as *obtain*, *activate*, *discard*, etc. *Karel J Robot* is another example.

91

In a different direction, you can also use the examples and exercises that you present to introduce larger, deeper ideas. The three case studies here are from different fields and would typically be covered in detail in other courses. It is good, however, to introduce these big concepts early on so that, for example, the compiler course isn't the first place students encounter parsing. Even when the treatment is shallow, it has benefit in increasing the student's range of knowledge. It can make them hungry for more.

If you want to use the projects presented here in your own courses, I have a couple of suggestions. The first is that you spend some time with them yourself. You will be better prepared for subtle issues that might arise and will have answered many of the questions that might arise before the students come up with them. You can also tailor them to your own use.

And for the story driven projects, you will be their customer. So think ahead about your own concept of the result and modify the stories accordingly. I wouldn't try to turn the stories into a complete specification, but you should be able to fill in as needed, and capture your responses both as tests and as additional stories as you go. You can, if you wish, give students a certain amount of leeway in what they do by letting them suggest stories.

Perhaps it is obvious, but the exercises and examples I use to teach programming in object-oriented languages are very different from what I used in the old Pascal/C days. Programs are larger and the students work within a defined framework, rather than building small, clever, things from scratch. The have code to read as well as write. Your student exercises can be larger than before, but if they are developed iteratively, you can have them do simpler things early. The difficulty will rise with their growing skills. I've long maintained that this is essential. The old things, like nim, and such, just won't do it. You may love those old, tricky, exercises, but they don't teach the lessons needed by *today's* students. To reprise the introduction to this book, it isn't your job to teach the students what *you* know, but what *they* need to know to survive professionally.

Teach it. Teach it good.

Notes

Accessor: A method that retrieves information from an object.

Accesso-Mutator: An occasionally necessary evil. A combination of Accessor and Mutator. Also, perhaps, Accessotator.

API: Application Programmer Interface. The methods available to a programmer other than the developer. The public methods of a class (among others, such as protected...)

CamelCase: Names that consist of words concatenated. Capitalize the words after the first. Also called BumpyWords.

Compiler: A program that translates an algorithm written in some language into an equivalent one in another language.

Dusty Deck: An old program that you have been tasked with updating. A holdover from the days of card readers.

Getter: Something to be avoided (or a personal assistant). See Accessor.

Grammar: A formal description of the structure of a language.

Interpreter: A program that takes a description of an algorithm written in some language and executes it. e.g. computer hardware.

Invariant: A property of an object that is maintained to be always true. The property is established by the constructor and maintained by every mutator. This also has a non-object interpretation.

Mutator: A method that updates an object, changing its state in some way.

Postorder: A tree processing method in which a node is processed after all of its children.

Setter: Something to be avoided (or a large dog). See Mutator.

Top Level: A class that is not an inner class. Normally appears in its own file.

Readings

Bergin: *Beyond Karel J Robot*, Joseph Bergin, Software Tools, 2008

Bergin: Introvert-Extrovert:
http://csis.pace.edu/~bergin/patterns/introvertExtrovert.html
and in *Pedagogical Patterns:Advice for Educators*

Brooks and many others: Quotes:
https://www.cs.cmu.edu/~pattis/quotations.html
http://www.csd.uwo.ca/faculty/hanan/quotes.html

Cockburn: Coffee Machine
http://alistair.cockburn.us/Coffee+machine+design+problem,
+part+1

Foote and Yoder: Big Ball of Mud:
http://www.laputan.org/mud/

Grossman and Bergin: Pair Story Telling,
http://csis.pace.edu/~bergin/xp/pairstorytelling.html

Homer: *The Iliad*, Translated by Robert Fagles, forward by Bernard Knox, Viking, 1990

Williams and Kessler: *Pair Programming Illuminated*, Addison-Wesley, July 2002

That's all, folks.

A pledge made to you
In the making of this work.
No haiku were harmed

www.ingramcontent.com/pod-product-compliance
Lightning Source LLC
LaVergne TN
LVHW052307060326
832902LV00021B/3749

* 9 7 8 1 9 4 0 1 1 3 0 6 7 *